Introducing Micronaut

Build, Test, and Deploy Java Microservices on Oracle Cloud

Todd Raymond Sharp

Apress®

Introducing Micronaut: Build, Test, and Deploy Java Microservices on Oracle Cloud

Todd Raymond Sharp
Blairsville, GA, USA

ISBN-13 (pbk): 978-1-4842-8289-2   ISBN-13 (electronic): 978-1-4842-8290-8
https://doi.org/10.1007/978-1-4842-8290-8

Managing Director, Apress Media LLC: Welmoed Spahr
Acquisitions Editor: Steve Anglin
Development Editor: James Markham
Coordinating Editor: Jill Balzano

Cover designed by eStudioCalamar

Cover image designed by Freepik (www.freepik.com)

Distributed to the book trade worldwide by Springer Science+Business Media New York, 1 New York Plaza, Suite 4600, New York, NY 10004-1562, USA. Phone 1-800-SPRINGER, fax (201) 348-4505, e-mail orders-ny@springer-sbm.com, or visit www.springeronline.com. Apress Media, LLC is a California LLC and the sole member (owner) is Springer Science + Business Media Finance Inc (SSBM Finance Inc). SSBM Finance Inc is a **Delaware** corporation.

For information on translations, please e-mail booktranslations@springernature.com; for reprint, paperback, or audio rights, please e-mail bookpermissions@springernature.com.

Apress titles may be purchased in bulk for academic, corporate, or promotional use. eBook versions and licenses are also available for most titles. For more information, reference our Print and eBook Bulk Sales web page at http://www.apress.com/bulk-sales.

Any source code or other supplementary material referenced by the author in this book is available to readers on GitHub or via the book's product page, located at www.springer.com/978-1-4842-8289-2.

Printed on acid-free paper

For Rhonda, Ribbÿ, and D-Bones.
You're my world and my inspiration.

Table of Contents

About the Author

Todd Sharp is a developer who advocates and evangelizes about Amazon Interactive Video Service at Twitch. He has been writing code since 2004 and feels extremely lucky to be paid to do what he loves and is truly passionate about. As part of his role as a developer advocate, he writes a lot of demo applications that show other developers how to use certain languages, frameworks, and technologies to solve the problems that they face every day. Todd has a background in writing and a love for theater, so he feels fortunate to have found a career that lets him use those skills and passions as part of his everyday routine. Todd is married to his best friend, and they live in the North Georgia mountains with their two kids, eight chickens, two dogs, a cat, and a potbelly pig named Milton. When he's not working, Todd loves to cook, play video games, and tinker with electronics and microcontrollers.

Acknowledgments

I'd like to acknowledge my appreciation of the following people who have helped me in my career. Without these folks, this book wouldn't be possible.

Gerald Venzl, for all your support and mentorship during my time at Oracle.

Graeme Rocher, for being a great friend and for patiently and expertly answering years of dumb questions and for creating some of the best frameworks that I've ever used. There are very few people in programming who think like you, and I will forever value your contributions and mentorship.

Raymond Camden and Scott Stroz, for putting up with me and being there for me whenever I need you. Love you, guys.

All the amazing engineers, product managers, project managers, and marketing and social team members whom I worked with during my time at Oracle. Thanks for making my time at Oracle special and fun. I'll never forget the time we spent together!

Finally, I'd never be the man that I am today without my beautiful wife, Rhonda. You've made me a better person and pushed me to be so much more than I ever dreamed of being. Thank you.

Introduction

Micronaut is a framework unlike many others in the Java world. Whether you've been writing Java code for 2 months or 20 years, you'll find it to be an easy-to-use framework that makes writing applications and microservices fun! But it's not just for Java developers! Maybe you use Kotlin or Groovy? No problem, because Micronaut supports those languages too!

In this book, we'll walk through building, testing, and deploying a REST-based microservice with Micronaut. We'll start with the very basics – creating the application and setting up a configuration file that will build our application with GitHub Actions. Next, we'll build and publish a JAR file. After that, we'll add some tests and ensure that those tests run during the build process and publish the results to the Web.

After we've created a JAR file and got our tests running, we'll deploy the application to a virtual machine (VM) on Oracle Cloud via the Oracle Cloud Infrastructure (OCI) Command-Line Interface (CLI). We'll also consider an alternative approach to deploying to the VM via the OCI Gradle plugin.

After we have deployed our simple service, we'll revisit the code and add a persistence tier with Micronaut Data and then test that persistence tier with Testcontainers. Finally, we'll redeploy the application to the cloud, but instead of deploying to a VM, we'll package the application in a Docker container and deploy it to a Kubernetes cluster.

I hope you enjoy reading this book as much as I enjoyed writing it. I believe Micronaut makes my life easier and makes writing applications more enjoyable, and I'm confident that you'll feel the same after reading this book.

CHAPTER 1

Creating a Micronaut Application and Getting Started with GitHub Actions

I have long been interested in build automation and continuous integration and continuous deployment (CI/CD). It's a topic that a lot of developers are interested in learning about, and it seems like there are constantly new tools to play with and learn about in the CI/CD world. And of course, as a developer advocate focused on the cloud and cloud DBs, that gives me a lot of content to play around with and talk to developers about.

With this in mind, join me on a long journey of short walks through the world of CI/CD over the next handful of chapters. We're going to look at building a simple microservice using some well-known technologies. We'll look at database migrations and testing our microservice as we go, and we'll ultimately end up deploying the app to Oracle Cloud.

© Todd Raymond Sharp 2022
T. R. Sharp, *Introducing Micronaut*, https://doi.org/10.1007/978-1-4842-8290-8_1

At first, we'll deploy to a VM instance. Then we'll look at bundling our microservice in a Docker container and deploying it on Kubernetes (also on Oracle Cloud). We'll handle all these operations with GitHub Actions as our tool to manage our build pipelines.

I know that I've laid out a long list of steps, but as I said we're going to focus on a single step per chapter in this book. In fact, let's start out in this very chapter by creating our simple microservice using Micronaut. You may already be familiar with the popular framework for creating performant and responsive microservices, but if not, you will soon see how easy it is to work with. That said, this book is more about CI/CD than it is about the microservice framework that we're going to use to build our microservice with. There are some specific features of Micronaut that we will take advantage of to make life easier, but everything we look at will be applicable in some manner to your applications regardless of the framework or language you're using.

Creating the Service

Let's create our service. With Micronaut, that's a matter of using the Micronaut CLI to scaffold out a basic service. If you don't already have the CLI installed, the following doc will provide you with the proper installation instructions depending on your OS:

https://micronaut-projects.github.io/micronaut-starter/latest/guide/#installation

Alternatively, you can utilize the Micronaut Launch tool to generate your project:

https://launch.micronaut.io

For my service, the CLI command that I used to create a service with the package name codes.recursive and the project name cicd-demo is

```
$ mn create-app codes.recursive.cicd-demo
```

```
| Application created at /Users/trsharp/Projects/apress/
cicd-demo
```

This results in the following application structure being created for us:

```
$ tree cicd-demo
cicd-demo
├── README.md
├── build.gradle
├── gradle
│   └── wrapper
│       ├── gradle-wrapper.jar
│       └── gradle-wrapper.properties
├── gradle.properties
├── gradlew
├── gradlew.bat
├── micronaut-cli.yml
├── settings.gradle
└── src
    ├── main
    │   ├── java
    │   │   └── codes
    │   │       └── recursive
    │   │           └── Application.java
    │   └── resources
    │       ├── application.yml
    │       └── logback.xml
    └── test
        └── java
            └── codes
                └── recursive
                    └── CicdDemoTest.java
```

You'll notice that by default the CLI gives us Gradle as our build tool. If you're more comfortable with Maven, simply add `--build maven` to the CLI command, and you'll end up with a `pom.xml` file instead of a `build.gradle` file. Please note though that if you use Maven instead of Gradle, you'll have to make some adjustments if you're following along with this book.

Before we move forward, open up the `gradle.properties` file in the root of the project and check the `micronautVersion`. If it's anything less than `3.0.2`, update it to at least that version.

Running the App

At this point, we have yet to write a single line of code, and yet we have an application ready to build. We can launch the application with `./gradlew run`, which results in the application running on `localhost:8080`:

```
$ ./gradlew run

> Task :run
```

```
  Micronaut (v3.0.2)

10:28:45.479 [main] INFO  io.micronaut.runtime.Micronaut -
Startup completed in 744ms. Server Running: http://
localhost:8080
```

Adding Support for GitHub Actions

Let's add our workflow configuration so that GitHub knows that we're
going to manage our builds with GitHub Actions.

Note   I'm not going to cover the basics of GitHub Actions in this
book, but rather I'll assume that you have a basic level understanding
of what it is and what it does. Please refer to the GitHub
documentation[1] if you want to learn more.

Now we'll create our workflow configuration file. It can be named
whatever you'd like but must end in .yml or .yaml and must reside in
the .github/workflows directory at the root of your project. The basic
hierarchy with GitHub Actions is Workflow ➤ Job ➤ Step. Workflows
have at least one job, and jobs contain steps to perform tasks like "build,
test, and package" – essentially, whatever you need to do to deploy your
application. Let's create our config file and call it cicd-workflow.yaml.
We'll populate it with a single step that just will echo a message to the
console:

```
name: cicd-demo
on:
  push:
    branches:
      - '*'
jobs:
  build-job:
    name: Build Job
```

---

[1]https://help.github.com/en/actions

```
runs-on: ubuntu-latest
steps:
  - name: 'Start build job'
    run: |
        echo "Starting the build job."
```

I'm using a wildcard (*) so that all branches are built in this example because I'm going to store each part of this book in a different branch. Now let's initialize a Git repo, add our files, and make our first commit:

```
$ git init
$ git branch -m master main
$ git add .
$ git commit -m "Initial Commit"
```

Next, we need to push the project to GitHub. I like to use IntelliJ's built-in support for this, so click Git ➤ GitHub ➤ Share Project on GitHub (Figure 1-1).

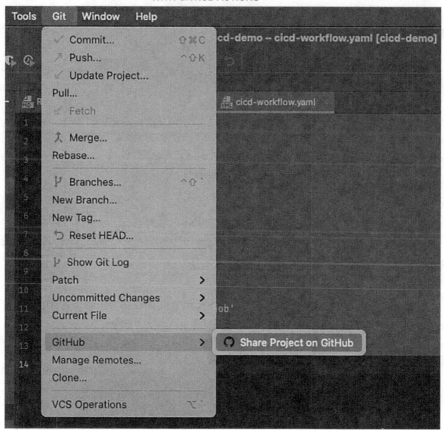

Figure 1-1. *Sharing the project to GitHub*

Note   I'm using IntelliJ IDEA 2021.2.2. Your version of IDEA may
have different menu entries.

Alternatively, you can manually create the project on GitHub and push
via the CLI:

```
$ git remote add origin [your repo URL]
$ git push -u origin main
```

At this point you can head to the project on GitHub and click the "Actions" tab (Figure 1-2).

Figure 1-2. *Navigate to the "Actions" tab*

This will list all the project workflows and a status of the latest runs for each (Figure 1-3).

Figure 1-3. *List the project workflows*

If you click the commit message, you can see a detailed log of the build output (which includes a live view while the build is running). Click each step for more information (Figure 1-4).

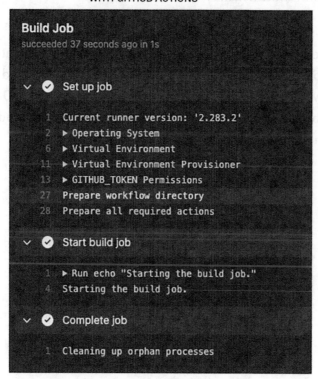

Figure 1-4. *Viewing the build output*

And with that, our very simple example has succeeded, and we have completed our very first build with GitHub Actions! Granted, it didn't do much in the way of building, testing, or deploying anything and the application had no meaningful code in it, but that's OK! We've taken the very first step, and we will build upon this foundation as we go forward adding relevant and helpful actions with each step.

Bling

I would be remiss if I didn't mention the fact that you can generate a super-awesome status badge for your builds that can be included in your README file, your team wiki, or wherever you'd like to include it. On the "Actions" tab, click the menu and select "Create status badge" and copy the generated markup (Figure 1-5).

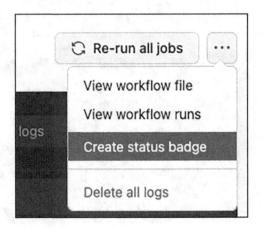

Figure 1-5. *Create a status badge*

You can paste this into your README, and your repo will always display the latest build status (Figure 1-6).

Figure 1-6. *Viewing the status badge on GitHub*

TL;DR

In this chapter we created a Micronaut project, checked it into GitHub, and created a basic GitHub Actions workflow configuration file. We pushed our code to GitHub and observed our first successful build.

Next

In the next chapter, we will dig deeper with GitHub Actions, install Java in our job runner, and build and publish our project artifacts.

Source Code

The source code for this chapter can be found at `https://github.com/recursivecodes/cicd-demo/tree/part-1`.

CHAPTER 2

Building and Publishing a JAR

In the last chapter, we created a Java microservice application, added our source code to a Git repository that was pushed to GitHub, and created a workflow configuration for GitHub Actions, which resulted in our first successful CI/CD run. Of course, that run didn't do anything except print out a message to the console, but it was successful nonetheless! In this chapter, we'll jump into more meaningful activities as it relates to CI/CD. Specifically, we'll focus on publishing an artifact (JAR file) for our microservice application.

Runners

Before we jump into this chapter, let's talk about how our CI/CD workflows get executed. GitHub Actions uses something called a "runner" to perform your workflow operations (see "Core Concepts for GitHub Actions"[1]). These are simply virtual machines that perform the operations that we tell them to via our configuration file. We can choose from Linux,

---

[1] https://help.github.com/en/actions/getting-started-with-github-actions/core-concepts-for-github-actions

© Todd Raymond Sharp 2022
T. R. Sharp, *Introducing Micronaut*, https://doi.org/10.1007/978-1-4842-8290-8_2

13

Windows, or macOS runners, and the runners come preconfigured with commonly used software (see the full list per operating system in the documentation[2]). We'll be using GitHub-hosted runners in this book, but you can also host your own runner[3] if your project has the need to do so.

Intro to "Actions"

The "Actions" part of GitHub Actions refers to the tool's ability to utilize bundled and preconfigured packages to perform certain operations within your workflow. At the time of this writing, there are over 3000 published actions[4] in the marketplace available for your workflows. These actions will make your builds easier by bundling common activities or simply installing a tool or utility into the runner environment so that it is available in your builds.

In our last chapter, we saw that our job step completed a task by using the run option in the step to execute a command on the runner:

```
steps:
  - name: 'Start build job'
    run: |
      echo "Starting the build job."
```

Many job steps will run commands like this, and others will utilize actions to perform certain activities (Figure 2-1). To use an action, visit the action's page in the marketplace and click "Use latest version" (or choose a specific version).

---

[2] https://help.github.com/en/actions/reference/software-installed-on-github-hosted-runners

[3] https://help.github.com/en/actions/hosting-your-own-runners

[4] https://github.com/marketplace?type=actions

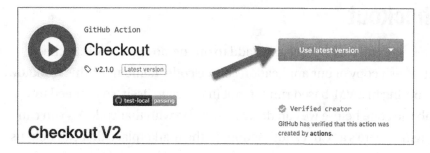

Figure 2-1. *The "Use latest version" button*

Then copy/paste the generated YAML into your workflow config file (Figure 2-2).

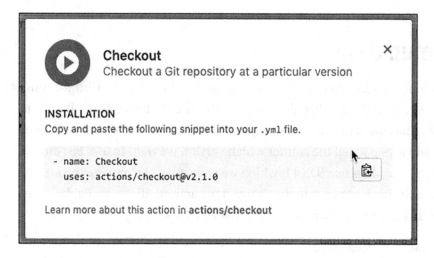

Figure 2-2. *The version checkout dialog*

Some actions accept input and produce output. We'll see more about that as we move forward.

Checkout

The first thing that we'll want to add to our demo workflow is to check out a fresh copy of our application source code. Remember, this workflow is running in a VM-based runner, not in our repo itself, so we need to grab the code before we can do anything else with that code. As you can imagine, there's a "Checkout" action[5] in the marketplace that can help us out with this. To use this action, we add the necessary YAML as a step for our job:

```
- name: 'Checkout'
  uses: actions/checkout@v2
```

Setup Java

To build our JAR file, we'll use Gradle (pre-installed in the Ubuntu runner), but we'll need a JDK installed to compile. The Ubuntu runner that we're using has the JDK pre-installed (versions 7, 8, 11, and 12), but we'll need to add a step to tell the runner which version we want to use. For our application let's use JDK 11, which we can specify by passing the input variable java-version to the setup-java action. All the available inputs for this action can be found in the action's docs[6]:

```
- name: 'Setup Java'
  uses: actions/setup-java@v1
  with:
    java-version: 11
```

---

[5] https://github.com/marketplace/actions/checkout
[6] https://github.com/actions/setup-java

And just to make sure:

```
- name: 'Check Java Version'
  run: |
    java --version
```

Progress Check

Let's commit and push to see how things are working so far:

```
git add . && git commit -m "Checkout code and Setup Java 11" &&
git push -u origin part-2
```

This kicks off our build, and our build runs successfully (Figure 2-3).

Figure 2-3. *The build output*

Building the JAR

So far, we're doing great! Everything is easy to configure; builds are running without failures. Life is good! Now that we have our source checked out to the runner workspace, let's build the JAR. Remember from our last chapter that we're using Gradle with our Micronaut application, so to create a JAR file, we invoke `./gradlew assemble,` which will build a JAR file and place it in the `build/libs` directory. We've already talked about Gradle being pre-installed on our runner VM, so we can simply add a step to invoke the `assemble` task with Gradle, and the JAR will be available in our workspace once it's complete:

```
- name: 'Assemble JAR'
  run: |
    ./gradlew assemble
```

Cool, so we have our first build artifact! Problem is once the job is complete, if we did nothing else, we would lose our JAR. It would simply go away since it's stored in the ephemeral storage on the runner VM. So we need to do something with the JAR after we build it.

Publishing the JAR

Ultimately, we're going to deploy our JAR to a production server (we'll look at a few different options for that later on in this book). But for now, let's simply "publish" the artifact, which is another way of saying "make the JAR available for download after the runner VM has terminated." Good news – there's an action that can help us with this! We'll want to add the current version number to the JAR's filename so that someone who downloads the artifact knows which version they are getting, so we'll add an interim step to grab that version number using Gradle and store it in an environment variable for use in subsequent steps. Here is the step to grab the version number:

```
- name: 'Get Version Number'
  run: |
    echo "VERSION=$(./gradlew properties -q | grep "version:" |
    awk '{print $2}')" >> $GITHUB_ENV
```

And here is the step to publish the JAR. The name key is what the published JAR will be named, and the path key is the path in the runner's workspace to the artifact that we want to publish. Since the JAR name changes with every version, we'll use a wildcard in the path to make sure we're always grabbing the latest JAR. Note that wildcard support was added to the upload-artifact action in v3-preview, so make sure you've got at least that version!

```
- name: 'Publish JAR'
  uses: actions/upload-artifact@v3-preview
  with:
    name: 'cicd-demo-${{env.VERSION}}-all.jar'
    path: build/libs/*-all.jar
```

At this point we can commit and push to kick off a new build:

```
$ git add . && git commit -m "Build & Publish JAR" && git
push -u origin part-2
```

This results in our JAR being built and our artifact being published. We can observe the build log to confirm (Figure 2-4).

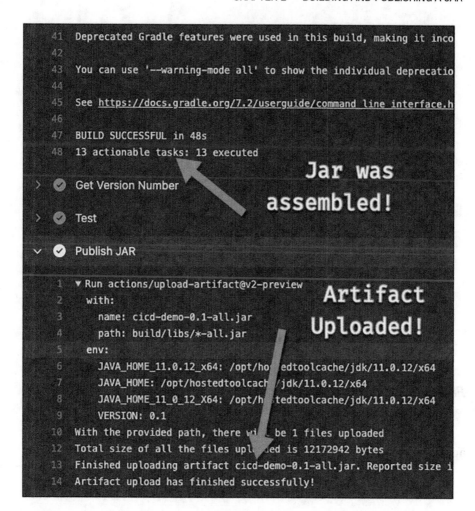

Figure 2-4. *The build log, confirming the JAR was built and the artifact was uploaded*

To download the JAR file, select "Summary" and download the file (Figure 2-5).

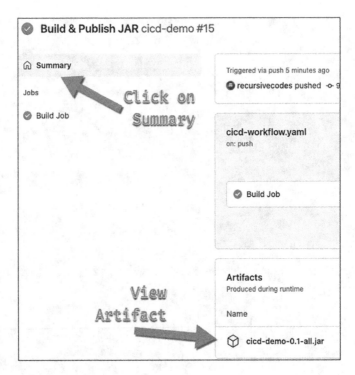

Figure 2-5. *The "Summary" link.*

At this point, we can download, unzip, and run the JAR file, and our application would start up (Figure 2-6).

Figure 2-6. *Running the generated artifact*

Note   In a public repo, any logged-in user can download your published artifacts. Keep this in mind and make sure this is your intention! Also note that published artifacts are different from GitHub "releases." If you wish to create a "release" for your project, check out the `create-release` action.[7]

TL;DR

In this chapter we talked about some GitHub Actions terminology and added some steps to our demo build to check out our code, configure Java on the runner VM, build a JAR file from our code, and publish that artifact so that it can be downloaded.

---

[7] https://github.com/actions/create-release

Next

In our next chapter, we will look at running tests and publishing the associated reports for those tests.

Source Code

The source code for this chapter can be found at `https://github.com/recursivecodes/cicd-demo/tree/part-2`.

CHAPTER 3

Running Tests and Publishing Test Reports

In this chapter we're going to look at tests, which are a crucial step to any proper CI/CD workflow. Certainly, your application already has a full suite of tests, and you're already used to making sure that these all pass before you deploy your application, so the theory (or "why") relating to tests should not be new to you. With that in mind, we'll focus on the "how" as it relates to tests in our demo project.

© Todd Raymond Sharp 2022
T. R. Sharp, *Introducing Micronaut*, https://doi.org/10.1007/978-1-4842-8290-8_3

Preparing Our App for Spock

Figure 3-1. *Leonard Nimoy as Spock, from the TV show Star Trek. NBC Television[1]/public domain*

I'm a big fan of using the popular Spock (https://spockframework.org/) library for testing as I feel that the expressive nature of the Groovy language makes writing tests easy and reading them even easier. To upgrade our Micronaut application to use Spock, let's modify our build.gradle file.

First, add the groovy plugin. Your plugins block should now look like this:

```
plugins {
    id("groovy")
    id("com.github.johnrengelman.shadow") version "7.0.0"
    id("io.micronaut.application") version "3.4.1"
}
```

---

[1] https://commons.wikimedia.org/wiki/File:Spock_at_console.jpg

Next, modify the `micronaut` block and change the `testRuntime` to spock2. Your `micronaut` block should now look like this:

```
micronaut {
    runtime("netty")
    testRuntime("spock2")
    processing {
        incremental(true)
        annotations("codes.recursive.*")
    }
}
```

Now let's add a dependency for the `micronaut-http-client` to the dependencies block:

```
testImplementation("io.micronaut:micronaut-http-client")
```

Finally, update `micronaut-cli.yml` in the project root to change the `testFramework` to spock instead of `junit`:

```
applicationType: default
defaultPackage: codes.recursive
testFramework: spock
sourceLanguage: java
buildTool: gradle
features: [annotation-api, app-name, gradle, http-client,
java, java-application, spock, logback, netty-server, readme,
shade, yaml]
```

Create a Spock Test

Since Spock uses Groovy, we need to create the proper directory structure in our `src/test` directory to contain our Spock tests (Figure 3-2).

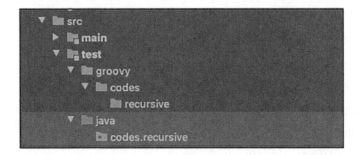

Figure 3-2. *The path to the directory where tests are created*

Since we're not going to use JUnit, delete the test located at /src/test/java/codes/recursive/CicdDemoTest.java that was created by default with our application (Figure 3-3).

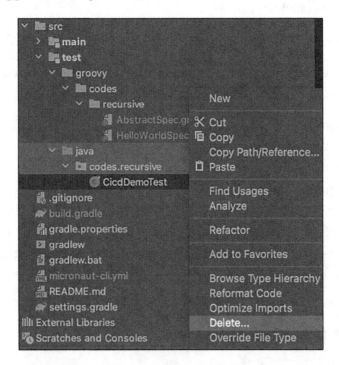

Figure 3-3. *Deleting the auto-generated JUnit test*

Within the src/test/groovy/codes/recursive directory, let's create a base test that our other tests will extend. It won't do much for now, but it'll come in handy later on:

```
package codes.recursive

import io.micronaut.context.ApplicationContext
import spock.lang.AutoCleanup
import spock.lang.Shared
import spock.lang.Specification

class AbstractSpec extends Specification {

}
```

Next, let's create a test! We don't have any application logic to test just yet, so create a simple HelloWorldSpec.groovy and populate it like so:

```
package codes.recursive

import io.micronaut.test.extensions.spock.annotation.
MicronautTest

@MicronautTest
class HelloWorldSpec extends AbstractSpec {

    def "test hello world"() {
        def foo = 'bar'
        when:
        foo == 'bar'
        then:
        foo.reverse() == 'rab'
    }

}
```

Now we can run the test locally with `./gradlew test`. It should quickly pass and produce a new report at `build/reports/tests/test/index.html` that you can view in your browser locally (Figure 3-4).

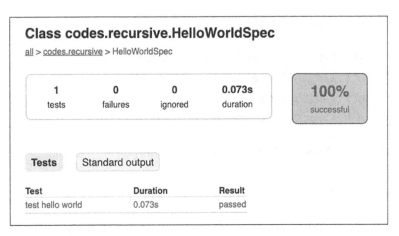

Figure 3-4. *The report*

Add a Controller and Test It

Let's add an actual controller to our microservice application so that we can run an actual, meaningful test. This is simple with the Micronaut CLI:

```
$ mn create-controller codes.recursive.controller.Hello
| Rendered controller to src/main/java/codes/recursive/
controller/HelloControllerController.java
| Rendered test to src/test/groovy/codes/recursive/controller/
HelloControllerControllerSpec.groovy
```

Since we updated the `micronaut-cli.yml` file earlier, Micronaut was kind enough to stub out a Spock test for us as it created our controller. Let's take a quick look at the controller it created:

package codes.recursive.controller;

```
import io.micronaut.http.annotation.*;

@Controller("/hello")
public class HelloController {

    @Get(uri="/", produces="text/plain")
    public String index() {
        return "Example Response";
    }
}
```

Nothing fancy at all, just a method that will return a "200 OK" response. What about the test that was generated? Note that the only change I made to the generated test was to extend my `AbstractSpec`:

```
package codes.recursive.controller

import codes.recursive.AbstractSpec
import io.micronaut.http.HttpResponse
import io.micronaut.http.HttpStatus
import io.micronaut.http.client.HttpClient
import io.micronaut.http.client.annotation.Client
import io.micronaut.runtime.server.EmbeddedServer
import io.micronaut.test.extensions.spock.annotation.MicronautTest
import jakarta.inject.Inject
import spock.lang.AutoCleanup
import spock.lang.Shared

@MicronautTest
class HelloControllerSpec extends AbstractSpec {

    @Shared @Inject
    EmbeddedServer embeddedServer
```

```
@Shared @AutoCleanup @Inject @Client("/")
HttpClient client

void "test index"() {
    given:
    HttpResponse response = client.toBlocking().
    exchange("/hello")

    expect:
    response.status == HttpStatus.OK
}
}
```

The generated spec includes an injected embedded server as well as an HttpClient that we can use to make requests to our controller. The single test makes a blocking request to the /hello endpoint and asserts that the response status is indeed "200 OK". Let's run our tests locally again (Figure 3-5).

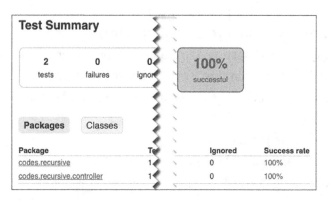

Figure 3-5. *The new test report*

Excellent! They all pass! Let's get these running in our build workflow!

Add an Action to Run Tests

I feel both sad and excited to tell you this next part. Excited because it's really simple and quick to run your tests with GitHub Actions and sad because there's not a fancy and clever way to do this. It's just a matter of executing a Gradle command to run the tests:

```
- name: 'Run Tests'
  run: |
      ./gradlew test
```

However, I am going to add this step above the "Assemble/Publish JAR" steps that we added in our last chapter because we want our build to fail if our tests are not passing.

Add an Action to Publish Tests

It would be extremely helpful if we publish our test reports so that we can view them offline after our build has run. This will help us troubleshoot failing tests and view the metric data for our tests. We can do this by using the same upload-artifact action that we used to publish our JAR file in the last chapter, so add another step to do this. Take note of the addition of the if key to this step definition, which allows us to run this step regardless of whether or not the previous steps have completed successfully. If we did not add this, our failed tests would effectively end the pipeline, and our test reports would not get published (potentially making it quite difficult to know why the tests failed!):

```
- name: 'Publish Test Report'
  if: always()
  uses: actions/upload-artifact@v2-preview
```

```
with:
  name: 'test-report'
  path: build/reports/tests/test/*
```

If we push this latest change to GitHub, our build will trigger, and we can observe the tests running (Figure 3-6) and our reports being published (Figure 3-7).

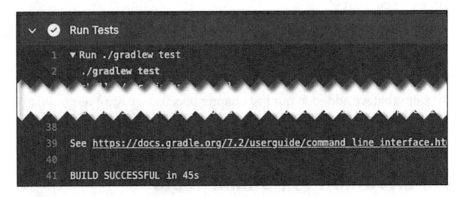

Figure 3-6. *The GitHub build output, confirming the test run*

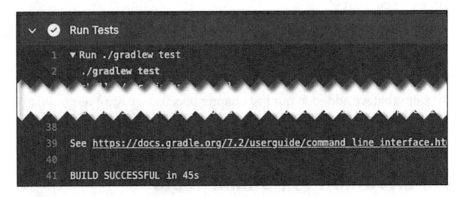

Figure 3-7. *The GitHub build output, confirming that the test report was published*

And we can confirm the published test report (Figure 3-8).

Artifacts
Produced during runtime

Name	Size
⬡ cicd-demo-0.1-all.jar	12.9 MB
⬡ test-report	19.9 KB

Figure 3-8. *The artifacts produced by the build, showing the published test report*

When Failure Happens

I know this never happens to you, but sometimes when I write tests, I end up getting some failures. Yeah, I know I should be embarrassed! So what would happen in our GitHub workflow if a failed test somehow slipped through the cracks and made it into our build? Well, let's intentionally write one to see what happens. I'll add the following to my HelloWorldSpec:

```
def "test failure"() {
    when:
    true == true
    then:
    false == true
}
```

And I'll push it to the branch I have been working with.

As you can see in Figure 3-9, the failed tests result in the overall build job failure, which prevents the creation and publishing of our JAR file but does not prevent the test report from being published, which means that we can still download that report to see what went wrong (Figure 3-10).

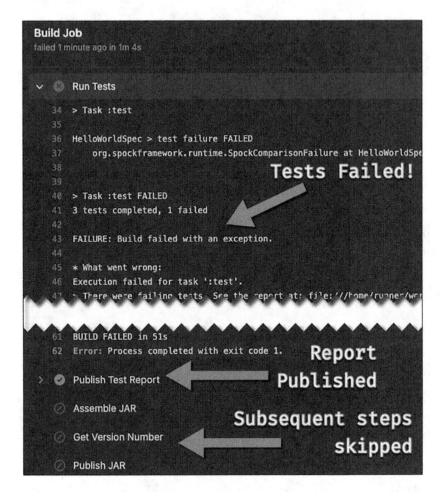

Figure 3-9. *GitHub build output showing failed tests*

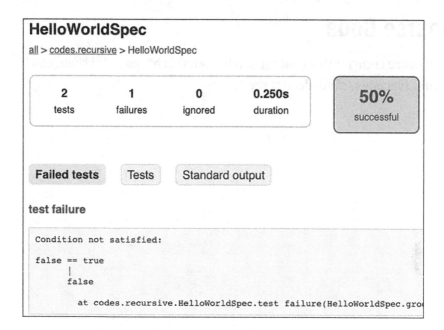

Figure 3-10. Failed test report

TL;DR

In this chapter we added some simple tests to our application and modified our workflow to run those tests and produce artifacts containing the results of the tests. We observed a successful run of the workflow with the tests as well as saw what happened when our tests did not pass.

Next

In our next chapter, we will jump into deploying our application to a virtual machine on Oracle Cloud.

Source Code

The source code for this chapter can be found at `https://github.com/ recursivecodes/cicd-demo/tree/part-3`.

CHAPTER 4

Deploying a Microservice to Oracle Cloud with GitHub Actions and the OCI CLI

We've made it to Chapter 4 in this book, which is where we finally get to deploy our microservice application to a virtual machine on Oracle Cloud. I know it may seem like it has taken us a long time to get to this point, but we've covered some very important material so far that has laid the foundation for us to be at the point we are at now. Our first version of our deployment will utilize the Oracle Cloud Infrastructure (OCI) Command-Line Interface (CLI) to create a VM in the cloud.

© Todd Raymond Sharp 2022
T. R. Sharp, *Introducing Micronaut*, https://doi.org/10.1007/978-1-4842-8290-8_4

Note   We're going to be working with the Oracle Cloud Infrastructure
(OCI) Command-Line Interface (**CLI**) and Software Development Kit
(**SDK**) as we move forward in this book. This means you will need
some information about your cloud tenancy and other items such as
public/private key pairs handy. If you have not yet configured the OCI
CLI on your local machine, you may want to do that now or simply
refer to the documentation[1] on how to do so to find some of the data
that we'll require in our GitHub Actions workflow.

Can You Keep a Secret?

We're going to be using the OCI CLI to create (or ensure the existence of)
the cloud infrastructure required to deploy our microservice application.
In order to use the CLI, we're going to need to first make sure that it is
installed on the runner VM and, second, we're going to need to create
the necessary config file on the runner VM that is used by the CLI to
authenticate our requests. To store the information required to create the
config file, we're going to use GitHub secrets.

Secrets are environment variables that are encrypted and only exposed
to selected actions. Anyone with collaborator access to this repository can
use these secrets in a workflow.

Let's create our secrets! Remember, all the data we need here is available
in your existing OCI CLI config file (usually located at ~/.oci/config).
To get started, go to the "Settings" tab in your project at GitHub and click
"Secrets" in the sidebar and then click "Add a new secret" (Figure 4-1).

---

[1]https://docs.cloud.oracle.com/en-us/iaas/Content/API/SDKDocs/
cliinstall.htm

Figure 4-1. *How to add a new secret to your GitHub repo*

Let's create secrets for the following credentials:

- User OCID

- Key fingerprint

- Key passphrase

- Tenancy OCID

- Region

- Key file contents

I like to prefix the secrets so that as I add additional secrets to my project for other purposes, it is easier to tell what the secret is being used for, so I'll prefix these secrets with OCI (Figure 4-2).

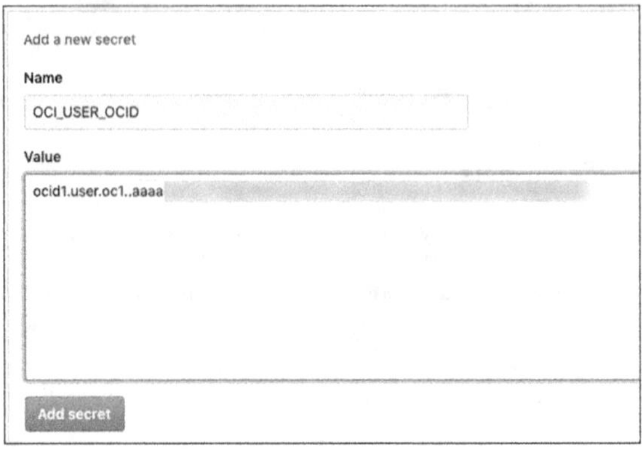

Figure 4-2. *The "Add a new secret" form*

Continue until you have all the necessary values configured as secrets in your GitHub project (Figure 4-3).

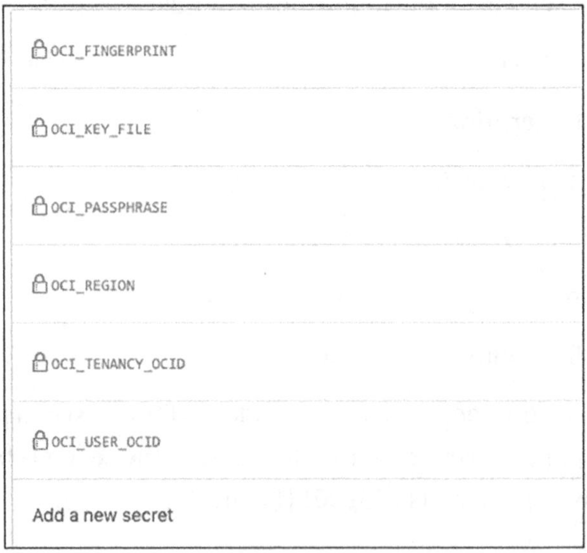

Figure 4-3. *The list of existing secrets after adding them to the GitHub project*

Using Secrets in Your Workflow

Using the GitHub secrets in your workflow is quite straightforward as
they are available in a "secrets" context that can be accessed from your
workflow (don't worry; sensitive secret values will be properly masked in
the console output). That means we can easily grab them and write out a
config file, so let's add a step to do that:

```
- name: 'Write Config & Key Files'
  run: |
    mkdir ~/.oci
    echo "[DEFAULT]" >> ~/.oci/config
    echo "user=${{secrets.OCI_USER_OCID}}" >> ~/.oci/config
    echo "fingerprint=${{secrets.OCI_FINGERPRINT}}" >>
    ~/.oci/config
    echo "pass_phrase=${{secrets.OCI_PASSPHRASE}}" >>
    ~/.oci/config
    echo "region=${{secrets.OCI_REGION}}" >> ~/.oci/config
    echo "tenancy=${{secrets.OCI_TENANCY_OCID}}" >>
    ~/.oci/config
    echo "key_file=~/.oci/key.pem" >> ~/.oci/config
    echo "${{secrets.OCI_KEY_FILE}}" >> ~/.oci/key.pem
    echo "${{secrets.VM_SSH_PUB_KEY}}" >> /home/runner/.oci/
    id_vm.pub
```

Installing the CLI

We can install the CLI via the provided install shell script, making sure to
pass the --accept-all-defaults flag so that the script does not wait for
any user input:

```
- name: 'Install OCI CLI'
```

```
run: |
  curl -L -O https://raw.githubusercontent.com/oracle/oci-
  cli/master/scripts/install/install.sh
  chmod +x install.sh
  ./install.sh --accept-all-defaults
  echo "/home/runner/bin" >> $GITHUB_PATH
  exec -l $SHELL
```

At this point, we've written our config file and SSH key to the runner's disk and installed the CLI. The only step left is to fix the permissions on those files so we can use the CLI:

```
- name: 'Fix Config File Permissions'
  run: |
    oci setup repair-file-permissions --file /home/runner/.
    oci/config
    oci setup repair-file-permissions --file /home/runner/.
    oci/key.pem
```

We can now use the CLI to perform any operation that we need to provision and deploy our microservice.

Creating the Instance

We can now move on to creating our VM instance. We will need some information in order to create our instance via the CLI, so create some more secrets containing the proper values for the following elements. Table 4-1 provides a quick overview of the necessary secrets for creating and working with a VM instance.

Table 4-1. *Secrets necessary to create the instance in our workflow*

Secret	Description
VM_AVAILABILITY_DOMAIN	The Availability Domain in which the instance will reside.
VM_COMPARTMENT_OCID	The compartment in which to create the instance.
VM_CUSTOM_IMAGE_OCID	An OCID for a custom image to use to create the VM – in my case, a custom image that has Java 11 pre-installed.
VM_SHAPE	The shape you want to use for the VM, for example: VM.Standard.A1.Flex.
VM_SSH_PRIVATE_KEY	The text content of an SSH private key that will be used to connect to the running instance to perform remote commands and to push the JAR file to the instance.
VM_SSH_PUB_KEY	The public part of the SSH key pair used to connect to the new instance.
VM_SUBNET_OCID	The OCID of the subnet to associate the instance. This subnet should have a security list that has the proper ingress rules in place to expose the necessary ports for your application.

Set the proper values into secrets as shown previously. We'll assume that your Virtual Cloud Network has been set up and configured outside of the build process. If necessary, you could use the CLI to provision one during your build.

Before we try to create our new instance, we should first check to see if the instance hasn't already been created (in a previous run). If it exists, we'll use that instance; but if it does not yet exist, we will create it. Let's add a step to our workflow configuration to perform this check via the CLI:

```
- name: 'Check Existing Instance'
  run: |
    echo "INSTANCE_OCID=$( \
      oci compute instance list \
      --lifecycle-state RUNNING \
      --compartment-id ${{secrets.VM_COMPARTMENT_OCID}} \
      --display-name cicd-demo \
      --query "data [0].id" \
      --raw-output \
    )" >> $GITHUB_ENV
```

Now we can create a conditional step to create the instance if it does
not yet exist. We simply add in if to check for the INSTANCE_OCID that
would have been set into the environment variables in the previous step:

```
- name: 'Create Instance'
  if: ${{!env.INSTANCE_OCID}}
  run: |
    echo "INSTANCE_OCID=$( \
      oci compute instance launch \
        -c ${{secrets.VM_COMPARTMENT_OCID}} \
        --availability-domain ${{secrets.VM_AVAILABILITY_
        DOMAIN}} \
        --shape ${{secrets.VM_SHAPE}} \
        --shape-config '{"memoryInGBs": 4, "ocpus": 1}' \
        --assign-public-ip true \
        --display-name cicd-demo \
        --image-id ${{secrets.VM_CUSTOM_IMAGE_OCID}} \
        --ssh-authorized-keys-file /home/runner/.oci/id_
        vm.pub \
        --subnet-id ${{secrets.VM_SUBNET_OCID}} \
        --wait-for-state RUNNING \
```

```
--query "data.id" \
--raw-output \
)" >> $GITHUB_ENV
```

Since the "Create Instance" step only runs if there is no `INSTANCE_OCID` in our environment, we need to make sure that we set it as a result of the new instance creation here so that we can use it in subsequent steps. Also note that we have added `–wait-for-state RUNNING` to the Create Instance call, which means it will block our pipeline execution until the instance exists. This is important since we wouldn't be able to work with it going forward unless it is up and running.

Deploy the App

So now that we have an instance created and up and running, we're ready to deploy our application to the running instance. We're going to use a few different "actions" from the marketplace – one to send remote commands via SSH and another to securely transfer our JAR file to the instance. To use those, we're going to need the instance IP, so add a step to our build pipeline to grab the public IP:

```
- name: 'Get Instance IP'
  run: |
    echo "INSTANCE_IP=$( \
      oci compute instance list-vnics \
      --instance-id ${{env.INSTANCE_OCID}} \
      --query 'data [0]."public-ip"' \
      --raw-output \
    )" >> $GITHUB_ENV
```

Wait for SSH

The instance may be in a "RUNNING" state after we created it earlier, but that doesn't mean that the OS is up and ready for connections just yet, so let's add a step to make sure we can connect via SSH before we move forward:

```
- name: 'Wait for SSH'
  run: |
    while ! nc -w5 -z ${{ env.INSTANCE_IP }} 22; do
           sleep 5
           echo "SSH not available..."
    done; echo "SSH ready!"
```

Stop App

Before we push our JAR file, let's stop the running application on the server. We'll use the SSH Remote Commands[2] action for this, which lets us execute these commands over SSH. This means we'll need our username and the private key associated with the public key we used earlier to create our instance (you should have already set this into your secrets if you followed the preceding steps). This next command will find the PID of the running application and kill that PID. Then it will create a directory for our application deployment to make sure it exists:

```
- name: 'Stop App'
  uses: appleboy/ssh-action@v0.1.4
  with:
    host: ${{env.INSTANCE_IP}}
```

---

[2] https://github.com/marketplace/actions/ssh-remote-commands

48

```
username: opc
key: ${{secrets.VM_SSH_PRIVATE_KEY}}
script: |
  pid=`ps aux | grep "[c]icd-demo.jar" | awk '{print $2}'`
  if [ "$pid" == "" ]; then
    echo "Process not found"
  else
    kill -9 $pid
  fi
  sudo mkdir -p /app
```

Push JAR

Now that the application has been shut down, we can push our JAR file.
For this we'll use the SCP Command action, passing the source file from
our runner VM's workspace build directory into the target app directory
that we created in the previous step:

```
- name: 'Push JAR'
  uses: appleboy/scp-action@v0.1.4
  with:
    host: ${{ env.INSTANCE_IP }}
    username: opc
    key: ${{ secrets.VM_SSH_PRIVATE_KEY }}
    source: "build/libs/cicd-demo-${{env.VERSION}}-all.jar"
    target: "app"
    strip_components: 2
```

Start App

The last step in our deployment is to restart the app now that the latest version has been uploaded. We'll use the Remote Commands action again, and this time I'll rename the uploaded JAR and make sure to use nohup so that the java -jar command continues to run after we disconnect and capture the output into a timestamped log file:

```
- name: 'Start App'
  uses: appleboy/ssh-action@v0.1.4
  with:
    host: ${{ env.INSTANCE_IP }}
    username: opc
    key: ${{ secrets.VM_SSH_PRIVATE_KEY }}
    script: |
      sudo mv ~/app/cicd-demo-${{env.VERSION}}-all.jar /app/
      cicd-demo.jar
      nohup java -jar /app/cicd-demo.jar > output.$
      (date --iso).log 2>&1 &
```

Run the Build

Once we've configured all our build steps, we can commit and push our code to GitHub to watch the magic happen (Figure 4-4).

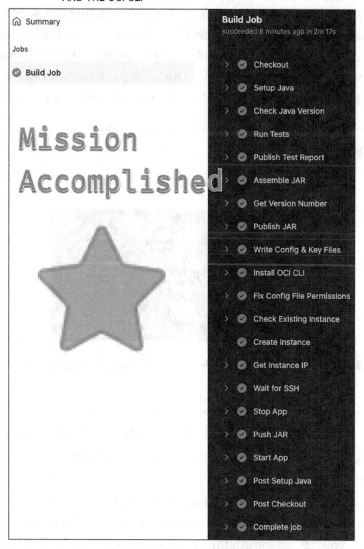

Figure 4-4. The build job, successfully deployed

We can confirm that the deployment was successful by making a cURL call (Figure 4-5) to our microservice. But before we can do that, we need to manually SSH into the instance and open port 8080 on the OS firewall (this command cannot be sent remotely). This must be done only once, as the rule will be permanent and the VM will be reused in subsequent builds:

```
$ sudo firewall-cmd --permanent --zone=public --add-port=8080/tcp
$ sudo firewall-cmd --reload
```

```
trsharp at ora-recursivecodes-mb in /tmp
$ curl -i 129.146.162.101:8080/hello
HTTP/1.1 200 OK
date: Sat, 16 Oct 2021 19:07:30 GMT
Content-Type: text/plain
content-length: 16
connection: keep-alive

Example Response
```

Figure 4-5. *Testing a response from the deployed application*

Note   If you cannot access the microservice at this point, make sure that your subnet has an ingress rule to allow port 8080.[3]

And from here on out, we can enjoy the beauty of CI/CD. Make a change, commit the code, and observe our automated deployment. Obviously, you'd wrap some additional logic around the process, but this book is about giving you the basic foundations on which to build.

---

[3] https://docs.oracle.com/en-us/iaas/Content/Network/Concepts/securitylists.htm

Let's add another controller method, commit, and push our code:

```
@Get("/version")
public HttpResponse<Map> getVersion() {
    return HttpResponse.ok(
            Map.of(
                    "version", "0.1"
            )
    );
}
```

After our pipeline runs, we can test the new endpoint (Figure 4-6).

```
trsharp at ora-recursivecodes-mb in ~
$ curl -s 129.146.162.101:8080/hello/version | jq
{
    "version": "0.1"
}
```

Figure 4-6. *Testing the new endpoint*

TL;DR

Wow, we covered a lot in this chapter, but it's all great stuff! In this chapter
we installed and configured the Oracle Cloud Infrastructure Command-
Line Interface (OCI CLI) into our GitHub Actions runner VM and then
used the CLI to conditionally create a VM instance on Oracle Cloud.
We then remotely stopped our microservice application on the cloud
instance, pushed our new JAR, and then remotely started our microservice
application.

Next

In our next chapter, we will consider an alternative method for deploying our microservice application to Oracle Cloud by using a Gradle plugin to perform the same activities instead of using the OCI CLI.

Source Code

The source code for this chapter can be found at `https://github.com/recursivecodes/cicd-demo/tree/part-4`.

CHAPTER 5

Deploying a Microservice to Oracle Cloud with GitHub Actions and the OCI Gradle Plugin

We've made it to Chapter 5 in this book, and I have to say that I'm having more fun than I should be allowed to have playing around with CI/CD and deploying microservices to Oracle Cloud. I have learned a ton putting this book together, and I truly hope you are enjoying it and finding it useful.

In that last chapter, we used the OCI CLI to create our instance, but this time we're going to switch our application to use the OCI Java SDK Gradle plugin[1] by my esteemed colleague Andres Almiray.[2] You'll need many of the secrets from the previous chapter created in your repo, so if you haven't created them yet, then you might want to do that now.

---

[1] http://kordamp.org/oci-gradle-plugin
[2] https://blogs.oracle.com/author/e475065c-7c0f-4efc-98f4-7d6d0212138d

© Todd Raymond Sharp 2022
T. R. Sharp, *Introducing Micronaut*, https://doi.org/10.1007/978-1-4842-8290-8_5

Configure Gradle

First, we will need to add the OCI Gradle plugin to our `build.gradle` file in the plugins block:

```
id 'org.kordamp.gradle.base' version '0.47.0'
id 'org.kordamp.gradle.oci' version '0.5.0'
```

We'll need to make sure that our Gradle wrapper uses version 7.1, so open /gradlew/wrapper/wrapper.properties and make sure that the distributionUrl is pointing at 7.1:

```
distributionBase=GRADLE_USER_HOME
distributionPath=wrapper/dists
distributionUrl=https\://services.gradle.org/distributions/
gradle-7.1-bin.zip
zipStoreBase=GRADLE_USER_HOME
zipStorePath=wrapper/dists
```

Since the plugin utilizes the OCI Java SDK, which depends on `javax.activation,` we'll need to add a `buildscript` dependency:

```
buildscript {
    repositories {
        mavenCentral()
    }
    dependencies {
        classpath 'com.sun.activation:jakarta.activation:1.2.2'
    }
}
```

Next, we'll register a new task in our build that we can later invoke from our build pipeline. We'll pass in the necessary variables from the pipeline, so register the task like so in your `build.gradle`:

```
/* default project properties to keep intellij from annoying me
with warnings */
if(! hasProperty("publicKeyFile")){
    ext.publicKeyFile=""
}
if(! hasProperty("userDataFile")){
    ext.userDataFile=""
}
def step01 = tasks.register('step01', org.kordamp.gradle.
plugin.oci.tasks.instance.SetupInstanceTask) {
    verbose       = true
    image         = 'java-11-custom-image'
    shape         = 'VM.Standard.E2.1'
    publicKeyFile = file("${project.publicKeyFile}")
    userDataFile  = file("${project.userDataFile}")
}
```

This task will utilize the SetupInstanceTask[3] method of the plugin,
and as I said previously, we will be able to pass additional variables in
when we execute the task later on. Let's move to our workflow yaml file and
remove the references to the OCI CLI that we added in the last chapter in
this book. Remove the steps with the following names:

```
- name: 'Install OCI CLI'
- name: 'Fix Config File Permissions'
- name: 'Check Existing Instance'
- name: 'Create Instance'
- name: 'Get Instance IP'
```

---

[3] http://kordamp.org/oci-gradle-plugin/#setupInstance

We'll still need our OCI config file as it will be used for authentication by the Gradle plugin, so leave that step in and add another command at the end of it to create a blank cloud-init file. We won't populate it for now, but if you wanted to further customize your newly launched instance, you could certainly populate this shell script (or have a version checked in to your GitHub repo that you could copy over):

```
- name: 'Write Config & Key Files'
  run: |
    mkdir ~/.oci
    echo "[DEFAULT]" >> ~/.oci/config
    echo "user=${{secrets.OCI_USER_OCID}}" >> ~/.oci/config
    echo "fingerprint=${{secrets.OCI_FINGERPRINT}}" >>
    ~/.oci/config
    echo "pass_phrase=${{secrets.OCI_PASSPHRASE}}" >>
    ~/.oci/config
    echo "region=${{secrets.OCI_REGION}}" >> ~/.oci/config
    echo "tenancy=${{secrets.OCI_TENANCY_OCID}}" >>
    ~/.oci/config
    echo "key_file=~/.oci/key.pem" >> ~/.oci/config
    echo "${{secrets.OCI_KEY_FILE}}" >> ~/.oci/key.pem
    echo "${{secrets.VM_SSH_PUB_KEY}}" >> /home/runner/.oci/
    id_vm.pub
    touch /home/runner/cloud-init.sh
```

Now let's add a step to use Gradle to invoke the task that we registered previously. Note that the Create Instance task will also create all the necessary VCN infrastructure to support the instance:

```
- name: 'Create Instance'
  run: |
    ./gradlew --stacktrace step01 \
      -Doci.compartment.id=${{secrets.VM_COMPARTMENT_OCID}} \
```

```
-Doci.instance.name=cicddemo2 \
-PpublicKeyFile=/home/runner/.oci/id_vm.pub \
-PuserDataFile=/home/runner/cloud-init.sh
```

This step will complete successfully regardless of whether the instance
exists beforehand, so we don't have to worry about checking that our
instance already exists before we invoke it. It will also write out a properties
file containing relevant data about the instance that we can use to get
information like our instance's public IP, so we've eliminated yet another
call to the CLI/SDK. That said, let's add a step to our workflow to read the
properties file and retrieve the instance IP as well as the security list ID so
we can add an ingress rule for the app that our microservice runs on:

```
- name: 'Get Instance IP'
  run: |
    more build/oci/instance/cicddemo2.properties
    function prop {
     grep "${1}" build/oci/instance/cicddemo2.properties|
     cut -d'=' -f2
    }
    echo "SECURITY_LIST_ID=$(prop 'vcn.security-list.id')" >>
    $GITHUB_ENV
    echo "INSTANCE_IP=$(prop 'instance.public-ip.0')" >>
    $GITHUB_ENV
```

Now we can add the ingress rule using the addIngressSecurityRule
task that the OCI Gradle plugin provides:

```
- name: 'Add Ingress Rule'
  run: |
    ./gradlew addIngressSecurityRule \
      --destination-port=8080 \
      --security-list-id=${{env.SECURITY_LIST_ID}}
```

From here on out, the build continues as it did in the previous
chapter. We can stop the app, push the JAR, and start the app with the
following steps:

```yaml
- name: 'Stop App'
  uses: appleboy/ssh-action@master
  with:
    host: ${{env.INSTANCE_IP}}
    username: opc
    key: ${{secrets.VM_SSH_PRIVATE_KEY}}
    script: |
      pid=`ps aux | grep "[c]icd-demo.jar" | awk '{print $2}'`
      if [ "$pid" == "" ]; then
        echo "Process not found"
      else
        kill -9 $pid
      fi
      sudo mkdir -p /app

- name: 'Push JAR'
  uses: appleboy/scp-action@master
  with:
    host: ${{ env.INSTANCE_IP }}
    username: opc
    key: ${{ secrets.VM_SSH_PRIVATE_KEY }}
    source: "build/libs/cicd-demo-${{env.VERSION}}-all.jar"
    target: "app"
    strip_components: 2

- name: 'Start App'
  uses: appleboy/ssh-action@master
  with:
    host: ${{ env.INSTANCE_IP }}
```

```
username: opc
key: ${{ secrets.VM_SSH_PRIVATE_KEY }}
script: |
  sudo mv ~/app/cicd-demo-${{env.VERSION}}-all.jar /app/
  cicd-demo.jar
  nohup java -jar /app/cicd-demo.jar > output.$
  (date --iso).log 2>&1 &
```

Once we commit and push our refactored build, we can observe the
workflow execution in GitHub Actions (Figure 5-1).

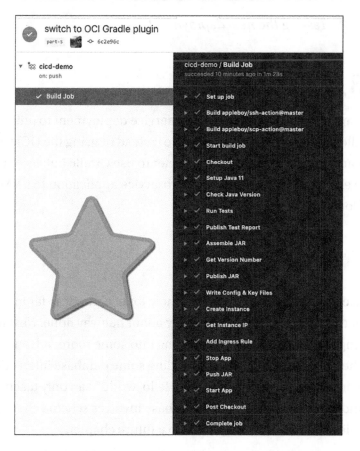

Figure 5-1. *The build output, after the refactored build*

And we can confirm the application has been deployed on the new
instance (Figure 5-2).

```
┌─trsharp@MacBook-Pro-5 ~
└─$ curl -i http://129.146.183.252:8080/hello
HTTP/1.1 200 OK
Date: Wed, 8 Apr 2020 17:42:19 GMT
connection: keep-alive
transfer-encoding: chunked

┌─trsharp@MacBook-Pro-5 ~
└─$ curl -s http://129.146.183.252:8080/hello/version | jq
{
    "version": "0.1"
}
```

Figure 5-2. *Testing the new deployment*

TL;DR

In this chapter we refactored our microservice deployment to utilize the
OCI Gradle plugin to create our instance instead of using the OCI CLI. This
presents an alternative option if you prefer to use Gradle but accomplishes
the same end goal – deploying our microservice application to a VM on
Oracle Cloud.

Next

I know it feels like we have covered a whole lot of content so far in this
book, but trust me when I say we're only about halfway done. Next up,
we're going to spend a few chapters going into some more "advanced"
topics. The first thing we'll look at is adding some database interactions
to our microservice because a simple "Hello, world" can only teach us so
much. And since working with the database involves schema changes,
we'll also look at database migrations in a future chapter.

Source Code

The source code for this chapter can be found at `https://github.com/`
`recursivecodes/cicd-demo/tree/part-5`.

CHAPTER 6

Adding a Persistence Tier to the Microservice

The logical path to take from here would be to add some database interactivity to our microservice application since that is certainly something that you'd need to do in any real-world project. We'll focus on adding a very simple persistence tier to the application that will store and retrieve user data to and from Oracle DB. Locally, we'll test against an instance of Oracle XE running in a Docker container, and we'll use Liquibase to handle our schema creation and migrations. This will make life much easier as our project grows larger, especially as we move on to testing and deploying the microservice with the persistence tier in place.

Managing Schema Modifications

It's pretty easy to track changes to our application code and share those changes with our distributed teams via source control. But tracking, managing, and applying changes to our database schemas is something that can be extremely challenging if your team does not use some sort of tool to help out with this sort of thing. Thankfully, we have several tools available to us to help with this task, and one of my favorite tools for that

© Todd Raymond Sharp 2022
T. R. Sharp, *Introducing Micronaut*, https://doi.org/10.1007/978-1-4842-8290-8_6

job is called Liquibase.[1] Liquibase is an open source library that works with just about every DB system you can imagine. It gives you the ability to define your schema changes in a specific XML file called a changelog that can then be executed against a DB to perform the necessary DDL operations to modify the schema or DML operations to modify data. This means your schema modifications can all be scripted and you never have to worry about manually running a query to modify a DB schema ever again. If you're not familiar with Liquibase, you can probably already see why it is a valuable tool to have in your toolbox.

Spin Up a DB

As we move forward in this book, we'll address the DB requirements for both test and production, but for now we're going to need a DB running locally to test against. My favorite method is to spin up Oracle XE in a Docker container, but you can follow your own favorite method to get a development DB spun up and ready to test your local instance against.

Note   Gerald Venzl has a great blog post that shows five ways to get an Oracle DB instance that you can access at `https://blogs.oracle.com/database/post/5-ways-to-get-an-oracle-database`. If you want to read about the latest (and easiest) method for an Oracle XE Docker container, check out `https://geraldonit.com/2021/08/15/oracle-xe-docker-images/`.

---

[1] `www.liquibase.org/`

Liquibase-Micronaut Integration

Adding Liquibase support to our microservice is pretty easy. We'll start off by adding a dependency for Liquibase to our build.gradle file:

```
implementation("io.micronaut.liquibase:micronaut-liquibase")
```

We'll also need to add some configuration to our application.yml file to tell Micronaut about our Liquibase integration so that it knows which file describes our changeset operations:

```
liquibase:
  datasources:
    default:
      change-log: 'classpath:db/liquibase-changelog.xml'
```

The next step is to create that changelog, so create a file called liquibase-changelog.xml within the src/main/resources/db directory (which you'll need to create). This file is a "master list" of your DB changes, which you will define in separate files as your schema evolves. Populate the changelog like so:

```
<?xml version="1.0" encoding="UTF-8"?>
<databaseChangeLog
        xmlns="http://www.liquibase.org/xml/ns/dbchangelog"
        xmlns:xsi="http://www.w3.org/2001/XMLSchema-instance"
        xsi:schemaLocation="http://www.liquibase.org/xml/ns/
        dbchangelog
         http://www.liquibase.org/xml/ns/dbchangelog/
         dbchangelog-3.8.xsd">
    <include
            file="changelog/01-create-user-table.xml"
            relativeToChangelogFile="true" />
</databaseChangeLog>
```

Note the <include> tag – we'll use one of these for each changeset as we move forward. Let's create that first one now. Create another directory, this one at src/main/resources/db/changelog, and add a file called 01-create-user-table.xml. This is the actual file that will tell Liquibase what exact changes we're looking to make against the database. There are commands to perform just about any operation that you can imagine – adding, dropping, and modifying of tables, views, sequences, and constraints. Whatever you need to do, it can be described in the XML format, which is interpreted and executed against your DB at runtime. And if you can't figure out the exact XML to define your change, you can always simply drop in raw SQL as needed!

Note   Liquibase also supports YAML, JSON, and SQL formats, and there is also a Groovy DSL and Clojure wrapper.

Here's how our first changeset looks. This file will result in the creation of a new table in our DB called users with an autonumber ID column and columns for first_name, last_name, email, and age:

```xml
<?xml version="1.0" encoding="UTF-8" standalone="no"?>
<databaseChangeLog xmlns="http://www.liquibase.org/xml/ns/
dbchangelog"
                   xmlns:xsi="http://www.w3.org/2001/XMLSchema-
                   instance"
                   xsi:schemaLocation="http://www.liquibase.
                   org/xml/ns/dbchangelog
http://www.liquibase.org/xml/ns/dbchangelog/dbchangelog-3.8.xsd">

    <changeSet id="01" author="toddrsharp">
        <createTable tableName="users"
                     remarks="A table to contain users">
            <column name="id" type="varchar(36)">
```

```
                <constraints nullable="false" primaryKey="true"
                primaryKeyName="users_pk" />
            </column>
            <column name="first_name" type="varchar(75)">
                <constraints nullable="false" />
            </column>
            <column name="last_name" type="varchar(75)">
                <constraints nullable="false" />
            </column>
            <column name="email" type="varchar(500)">
                <constraints nullable="true" />
            </column>
            <column name="age" type="number(3,0)">
                <constraints nullable="false" />
            </column>
        </createTable>
    </changeSet>
</databaseChangeLog>
```

Important!   Don't modify changelog/changeset files after they
have been run! If you need to change an action taken (e.g., delete
a column that was created in error), you'll need to add another
changeset to undo that previous schema modification.

If we were to run our application at this point, we wouldn't yet
see any DB modifications. Why? Because we haven't yet created any
datasources! Let's start working on that now by adding a configuration
for our development environment. We'll create a new file next to our
application.yml file and call it application-dev.yml. This file will
contain a datasource that will be associated with the "dev" profile that

we can activate by passing in an environment variable called MICRONAUT_
ENVIRONMENTS:

```
datasources:
  default:
    url: ${DATASOURCE_URL}
    driverClassName: oracle.jdbc.driver.OracleDriver
    connectionFactoryClassName: oracle.jdbc.pool.
    OracleDataSource
    username: ${DATASOURCE_USERNAME}
    password: ${DATASOURCE_PASSWORD}
    schema-generate: NONE
    dialect: ORACLE
```

Micronaut supports injecting configuration via environment variables
using the ${} syntax, which also supports a default value after the colon
in the declaration (IE: ${FOO:bar}). Let's set these environment variables
in our IDE so they'll be properly injected at runtime when we test locally
(Figure 6-1).

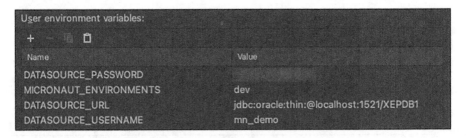

Figure 6-1. Adding environment variables in IntelliJ

Next, we'll add some database interactions.

Add Micronaut Data

Following the ongoing theme of this book, we're going to keep things very simple for the persistence tier itself by utilizing Micronaut Data.[2] What's Micronaut Data? Well, according to the documentation

---

Micronaut Data is a database access toolkit that uses Ahead of Time (AoT) compilation to precompute queries for repository interfaces that are then executed by a thin, lightweight runtime layer.

Essentially it is a very easy way to add persistence operations to a microservice. It will take your domain model objects and data repository interfaces that you create and annotate and automatically implement the necessary SQL for persistence operations. It's my favorite toolkit at the moment since it integrates so nicely with the Micronaut framework that we're already using, and it means I don't have to write a single line of SQL to get full CRUD operations in my microservice.

Add Dependencies

We'll need a few dependencies, so add them to our build.gradle file. These are the necessary libraries for Micronaut Data, the Oracle JDBC driver, and Hikari, which we'll use for connection pooling. Finally, we'll use the Jakarta Persistence library because it contains some familiar annotations that we can apply to our model class later:

```
annotationProcessor("io.micronaut.data:micronaut-data-
processor")
implementation("io.micronaut.data:micronaut-data-jdbc")
implementation 'com.oracle.database.jdbc:ojdbc11:21.1.0.0'
```

---

[2]https://micronaut-projects.github.io/micronaut-data/latest/guide/

```
implementation("io.micronaut.sql:micronaut-jdbc-hikari")
compileOnly("jakarta.persistence:jakarta.persistence-
api:2.2.2")
```

Note   Micronaut Data comes in four flavors: JDBC, JPA, R2DBC, and MongoDB. I like the simplicity of the JDBC flavor, but you can feel free to work with the JPA variety if you'd like to. Refer to the Micronaut Data documentation for more information.

Next, we need to slightly modify our Application class. Open up `Application.java` and modify it as shown in the following. We're setting a system property to prevent the Oracle driver from attempting to use FAN and slightly modifying the `Micronaut.run()` command to change the behavior on how environment variables are loaded for better performance:

```
public class Application {
    public static void main(String[] args) {
        System.setProperty("oracle.jdbc.fanEnabled", "false");
        Micronaut
                .build(args)
                .mainClass(Application.class)
                .environmentPropertySource(false)
                .start();
    }
}
```

Start the Application

At this point, we've configured our application enough that we can start it up and observe the Liquibase script execution to create our necessary table as outlined in our preceding changelog. Don't forget to set the proper environment variables (see the preceding code) before launching. Your console output should look like the following:

```
        Micronaut (v3.0.2)

12:42:35.965 [main] INFO  i.m.context.env.DefaultEnvironment -
Established active environments: [dev]
Oct 18, 2021 12:42:39 PM liquibase.lockservice
INFO: Successfully acquired change log lock
Oct 18, 2021 12:42:40 PM liquibase.changelog
INFO: Creating database history table with name: MN_DEMO.
DATABASECHANGELOG
Oct 18, 2021 12:42:40 PM liquibase.changelog
INFO: Reading from MN_DEMO.DATABASECHANGELOG
Oct 18, 2021 12:42:40 PM liquibase.changelog
INFO: Table users created
Oct 18, 2021 12:42:40 PM liquibase.changelog
INFO: ChangeSet db/changelog/01-create-user-table.
xml::01::toddrsharp ran successfully in 42ms
Oct 18, 2021 12:42:40 PM liquibase.lockservice
INFO: Successfully released change log lock
Oct 18, 2021 12:42:40 PM liquibase.lockservice
INFO: Successfully acquired change log lock
```

```
Oct 18, 2021 12:42:43 PM liquibase.changelog
INFO: Reading from MN_DEMO.DATABASECHANGELOG
Oct 18, 2021 12:42:43 PM liquibase.lockservice
INFO: Successfully released change log lock
12:42:44.646 [main] INFO  io.micronaut.runtime.Micronaut -
Startup completed in 8802ms. Server Running: http://
localhost:8080
```

As you can see, Liquibase has created a few tables to track its own operations and generated and executed the DDL to create our users table. We can confirm the creation by running a simple query (Figure 6-2).

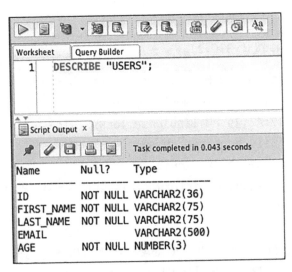

Figure 6-2. *Describing the "USERS" table in SQL Developer*

Let's pause here to recognize just how awesome this is. We haven't written a single line of SQL, yet we have a table created in our database in such a manner that as we move forward with our CI/CD pipeline, our test and production environments will recreate this schema without us having to even think about it!

As awesome as this is, I assure you it is about to get awesome-er.

Let's look at how to define our domain model entity and add persistence operations.

Create a Model

If you've written a Java application in the past, you know what a POJO looks like. Our domain model is a simple POJO with few annotations to let Micronaut Data know it needs to manage this entity.

To make life easier, we'll use Project Lombok so that we can avoid some of the verbose code usually required in a POJO. Let's add the dependencies for Project Lombok to our build.gradle. Add these at the **very beginning** of your dependencies block to avoid potential conflicts:

```
compileOnly 'org.projectlombok:lombok:1.18.12'
annotationProcessor "org.projectlombok:lombok:1.18.12"
```

Now create the domain class POJO. We'll annotate this POJO with @Entity so that Micronaut knows that this is a domain class that it needs to manage, @Table (since the domain class name differs from the actual table name), and @Data[3] so that Lombok generates the getters, setters, etc. that we need. Take note of the @Id annotation on our ID column. I hope that one is self-explanatory, but if not, it indicates which column is our ID column:

```
@Entity
@Table(name = "users")
@Data
public class User {
```

---

[3] https://projectlombok.org/features/Data

```
@Id
@AutoPopulated
private UUID id;
@NotNull
@Size(min = 3, max = 75)
private String firstName;
@NotNull
@Size(min = 5, max = 75)
private String lastName;
@Size(min = 1, max = 150)
private int age;
@Nullable
@Email
@Size(max = 500)
private String email;

public User(String firstName, String lastName, int age,
@Nullable String email) {
    this.firstName = firstName;
    this.lastName = lastName;
    this.age = age;
    this.email = email;
}
}
```

Create a Repository

The next step we need to take is to create a repository that will be used to expose our CRUD operations for our User object. Prepare yourself for something more awesome, because this one is pretty amazing. Here we simply define an interface that extends CrudRespository with the proper annotation to define the SQL dialect, and Micronaut Data will construct all the necessary CRUD queries behind the scenes at compile time, and they'll be ready for use immediately throughout the application. Create the file at repository/UserRepository.java and populate as such:

```
package codes.recursive.repository;

import codes.recursive.domain.User;
import io.micronaut.data.jdbc.annotation.JdbcRepository;
import io.micronaut.data.model.query.builder.sql.Dialect;
import io.micronaut.data.repository.CrudRepository;

import java.util.UUID;

@JdbcRepository(dialect = Dialect.ORACLE)
public interface UserRepository extends CrudRepository<User,
UUID> {}
```

That's it. That's the whole thing. At runtime we now get

- count()
- delete()
- deleteById()
- deleteAll()
- existsById()
- findAll()
- findById()
- save()
- saveAll()
- update()

All free of charge.

Modify the Controller

Let's modify our controller to add two methods: one to save a new user and one to return a user by ID. We'll first need to add a constructor and inject our repository:

```
private final UserRepository userRepository;
public HelloController(UserRepository userRepository) {
    this.userRepository = userRepository;
}
```

We should also update our application.yml file to run blocking operations on the I/O thread pool (see https://docs.micronaut.io/latest/guide/#threadPools):

```
micronaut:
  executors:
    io:
      type: fixed
      nThreads: 75
```

Then add the endpoints:

```
@Post("/")
public HttpResponse saveUser(@Valid User user) {
    return HttpResponse.created(
            userRepository.save(user)
    );
}

@Get("/{id}")
public HttpResponse getById(UUID id) {
    return HttpResponse.ok(
            userRepository.findById(id)
    );
}
```

Test Persistence

Let's launch our app and issue a few cURL commands to test out our progress so far:

```
curl -s -H "Content-Type: application/json" \
    -X POST \
    -d '{"firstName":"todd", "lastName":"sharp", "email":
    "me@ohmy.com", "age":42}' \
    http://localhost:8080/hello/ | jq
```

This should return the new user object:

```
{
    "id": "0d5985c4-6581-425e-abb2-624f0f8e9540",
    "firstName": "todd",
    "lastName": "sharp",
    "age": 42,
    "email": "me@ohmy.com"
}
```

And here's for the getById() method:

```
$ curl -s http://localhost:8080/hello/0d5985c4-6581-425e-
abb2-624f0f8e9540 | jq
```

This will return the same brand-new user as earlier:

```
{
    "id": "0d5985c4-6581-425e-abb2-624f0f8e9540",
    "firstName": "todd",
    "lastName": "sharp",
    "age": 42,
    "email": "me@ohmy.com"
}
```

TL;DR

In this chapter we added a lot of stuff! We added Liquibase for schema migrations and CRUD operations on a new domain model via a data repository and the necessary controller methods to persist data into a local Oracle DB.

Next

Next up, we're going to add some tests to ensure the quality of our persistence tier before we redeploy our application to production.

Source Code

The source code for this chapter can be found at `https://github.com/recursivecodes/cicd-demo/tree/part-6`.

CHAPTER 7

Testing the Persistence Tier with Testcontainers

Now that we've got a functional persistence tier in place, the next step is to update our workflow to deploy the application and any new dependencies to production, right? No, of course not! We haven't yet written the necessary tests to ensure a bug-free production build, so of course we'll focus on that in this chapter. But, since our CI/CD pipeline executes on GitHub's "runner" VMs, how can we test our persistence tier? Well, we could spin up an additional "test" database instance, but that could become costly over time and might become difficult to manage. The good news is that there's a better solution in the form of Testcontainers.[1] Let me borrow a bit of text from their homepage to explain what Testcontainers is:

> Testcontainers is a Java library that supports JUnit tests, providing lightweight, throwaway instances of common databases, Selenium web browsers, or anything else that can run in a Docker container. Testcontainers make the following kinds of tests easier: Data access layer integration tests: use a

---

[1] http://testcontainers.org/

© Todd Raymond Sharp 2022
T. R. Sharp, *Introducing Micronaut*, https://doi.org/10.1007/978-1-4842-8290-8_7

containerized instance of a MySQL, PostgreSQL or
Oracle database to test your data access layer code
for complete compatibility, but without requiring
complex setup on developers' machines and safe in
the knowledge that your tests will always start with a
known DB state.

How absolutely perfect and helpful is that?! With Testcontainers we can
spin up a full Oracle XE database that lives for the life of our tests and allows
us to test our microservice against the same Oracle DB that it'll end up being
deployed to when it reaches production. This will avoid any potential false
positives (and false negatives) that may arise from testing against something
like H2 instead of the same engine we're deploying to in production. OK, if
you're not as excited to dig into the fun as I am yet, then I'm not sure we can
be friends (or I may just be kinda weird – and that's certainly a possibility).

Adding Dependencies

We're going to need to grab the bits and bytes from Maven if we want to
use Testcontainers to spin up an Oracle DB instance and make sure that
our persistence operations work as we expect them to before we move
them to production. Let's get the Testcontainers Spock JAR and the JAR
necessary to work with Oracle XE DB:

```
testImplementation("org.testcontainers:spock:1.16.1")
testImplementation("org.testcontainers:oracle-xe:1.16.1")
```

Modifying Our Abstract Spec

If you remember back in Chapter 3 of this saga, we created an
AbstractSpec class that our other tests would extend. The reason we
created that was so when we got to this step, we'd be ready to simply

modify that base test to create our OracleContainer and initialize that container with the proper configuration so that our tests had an instance of Oracle XE in a Docker container up and running to query against. Let's make those modifications now:

Note   It's highly recommended that you use the gvenzl/oracle-xe:18-slim Docker image for your tests with Testcontainers for maximum performance!

```
class AbstractSpec extends Specification {
    @Shared
    @AutoCleanup
    static ApplicationContext context
    static {
        OracleContainer oracleContainer = new
        OracleContainer("gvenzl/oracle-xe:18-slim")
        oracleContainer.start()

        System.setProperty("oracle.jdbc.fanEnabled", "false")

        context = ApplicationContext.run(
                [
                            "datasources.default.connection-
                            factory-class-name": "oracle.jdbc.pool.
                            OracleDataSource",
                            "datasources.default.driver-
                            class-name": "oracle.jdbc.driver.
                            OracleDriver",
                            "datasources.default.url":
                            oracleContainer.getJdbcUrl(),
                            "datasources.default.username":
                            oracleContainer.getUsername(),
```

```
                        "datasources.default.password":
                        oracleContainer.getPassword(),
                        "datasources.default.schema-generate":
                        SchemaGenerate.NONE,
                        "datasources.default.dialect":
                        Dialect.ORACLE
            ],
            Environment.TEST
        )
    }
}
```

Take note that we're passing a path in the `OracleContainer` constructor to a valid Oracle XE Docker image (`gvenzl/oracle-xe:18-slim`[2]). You can use this image in your own tests if you'd like or enter your own path to a valid Oracle XE image. In the `static` block, we start the container and our `ApplicationContext`, passing the configuration for our datasource for the tests.

Now we can create tests that test out persistence activities and ensure that they'll properly execute in our test environment. Why is this awesome? Well, for starters, it means we don't have to turn up and pay for (and maintain) a "test" database environment just to run our tests against. Also, because we're using a container that's running Oracle DB, we are able to test against the same system that we will ultimately be deploying to in production (instead of testing against an in-memory H2 DB, e.g., that may or may not have full compatibility with our prod DB). Testing against our repo is simple. Let's add a `UserRepoSpec` that grabs our `UserRepository` bean, persists a new user, and then queries the DB to retrieve that user:

`@MicronautTest`

---

[2] https://hub.docker.com/r/gvenzl/oracle-xe

```
@Testcontainers
class UserRepoSpec extends AbstractSpec {
    @Inject UserRepository userRepository
    def "Can create a user"() {
        when:
        userRepository = context.getBean(UserRepository)
        User user = new User("Todd", "Sharp", 43, "todd.sharp@
        oracle.com")
        userRepository.save(user)
        then:
        userRepository.findById(user.getId()).get().getId() ==
        user.getId()
    }
}
```

Running the Pipeline Tests with Testcontainers

That's all the changes that we need to make to use Testcontainers in our project. We can run our tests locally to confirm and then push our changes to GitHub and watch our pipeline job utilize the new testing infrastructure (Figure 7-1).

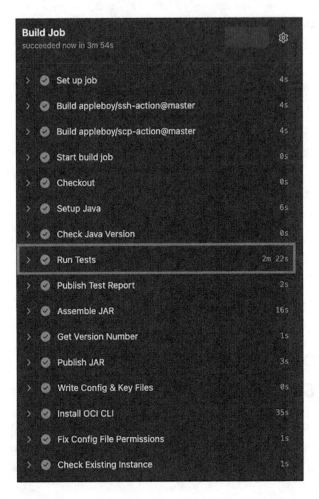

Figure 7-1. *Build output, highlighting the "Run Tests" step*

As we can clearly see, the job completed without errors, but it did take a bit longer than it did before. Specifically, the "Run Tests" step took slightly longer than it did before (Figure 7-2).

Figure 7-2. *The duration of the "Run Tests" step*

If you think about it, this makes sense. Testcontainers needs to pull the Docker image from my registry and then build and run the container. That means that the container needs to download and configure Oracle DB in the process, which does take a little bit of time!

> We're trading the monetary cost, unreliable results, and maintenance complexity for simplicity and reliability all for a price of a few short minutes. I'd say that's a fair trade.

At this point if you were to test the deployed application, you would notice that the persistence operations for this application are not yet working:

```
$ curl -s 129.146.98.229:8080/hello/a6b0416e-81d1-432f-
bdb8-92c1ab5edb9c | jq
{
    "message": "Internal Server Error",
    "_embedded": {
    "errors": [
            {
                "message": "Internal Server Error: No backing
                RepositoryOperations configured for repository.
                Check your configuration and try again"
            }
        ]
```

```
    },
        "_links": {
        "self": {
            "href": "/hello/a6b0416e-81d1-432f-bdb8-92c1ab5edb9c",
            "templated": false
        }
    }
}
```

This is because we haven't yet configured the proper datasource connectivity for our "production" instance. But that's another chapter, so we'll solve that issue next time!

TL;DR

In this chapter we added support for Testcontainers to our microservice application, wrote the proper tests to ensure our persistence tier was bug-free, and added the necessary support to our pipeline to execute the new tests.

Next

Next, we'll update our pipeline to deploy our fully tested microservice with a shiny, new persistence tier.

Source Code

The source code for this chapter can be found at https://github.com/recursivecodes/cicd-demo/tree/part-7.

CHAPTER 8

Deploying the Microservice with a Tested Persistence Tier in Place

In this chapter we're going to focus on the changes necessary to deploy our microservice now that we have added a persistence tier and tested it in our pipeline with Testcontainers. Since we used Liquibase to manage our DB migrations, it should be a pretty painless journey to deploy our application to Oracle Cloud. So far, we've got our application tested against Oracle XE both locally and in our pipeline, and we're confident that we're ready to deploy our changes to our "production" instance, which is currently set up as a VM on Oracle Cloud. We've yet to configure any database for production yet, so it's time to spin up an instance of Autonomous DB in the cloud. If you're new to Autonomous DB, here are several resources that will help you become familiar with it:

© Todd Raymond Sharp 2022

T. R. Sharp, *Introducing Micronaut*, https://doi.org/10.1007/978-1-4842-8290-8_8

- https://blogs.oracle.com/developers/the-
  complete-guide-to-getting-up-and-running-with-
  autonomous-database-in-the-cloud

- www.youtube.com/watch?v=5OZbr7AvLR4

Note   You don't have to use an Autonomous DB wallet to connect!
Instead, you can configure your database to use TLS and add an ACL
allow list for your DB instance. Read more here: `https://blogs.`
`oracle.com/developers/post/securely-connecting-to-`
`autonomous-db-without-a-wallet-using-tls`.

Autonomous Wallet

Our Autonomous DB connection requires the use of a "wallet" to make
a secure connection. The good news is that Micronaut includes support
for automatically downloading your wallet for you. We'll walk through the
necessary steps to configure this, but you might want to read this tutorial
for a full overview of the process:

https://blogs.oracle.com/developers/post/automatic-
autonomous-wallet-download-configuration-with-micronaut

You'll want to create a schema/user for the microservice application,
so connect to your Autonomous DB instance as your "admin" user and run
the following:

```
CREATE USER mn_demo IDENTIFIED BY "Str0ng_Password";
GRANT CONNECT, RESOURCE TO mn_demo;
GRANT UNLIMITED TABLESPACE TO mn_demo;
```

We can test the Autonomous DB connection locally, but to do that, you'll have to make sure that you have the OCI CLI[1] installed and configured.

Configure the Local Autonomous DB Datasource

We need to bring in the `micronaut-oracle-cloud`-specific dependencies, so let's add those to our `build.gradle`:

```
implementation("io.micronaut.oraclecloud:micronaut-oraclecloud-sdk:2.0.3")
implementation("io.micronaut.oraclecloud:micronaut-oraclecloud-atp:2.0.3")
```

We'll need to add a new configuration file, so create a new file in `src/main/resources` called `application-localadb.yml`. Populate this config file as follows:

```
datasources:
  default:
    driverClassName: oracle.jdbc.driver.OracleDriver
    connectionFactoryClassName: oracle.jdbc.pool.
    OracleDataSource
    ocid: ${DATASOURCE_OCID}
    walletPassword: ${DATASOURCE_WALLET_PASSWORD}
    username: ${DATASOURCE_USERNAME}
    password: ${DATASOURCE_PASSWORD}
    schema-generate: NONE
    dialect: ORACLE
```

---

[1]https://docs.oracle.com/en-us/iaas/Content/API/SDKDocs/cliinstall.htm

```
oci:
  config:
    profile: DEFAULT
```

Note the omission of the url property from our previous local datasource. Micronaut will determine that automatically for us and populate it. We've also added some new properties: ocid and walletPassword. The OCID represents the unique identifier assigned to your Autonomous DB instance, and you can obtain this via the OCI console. The walletPassword can be any password that you would like to use to encrypt the downloaded wallet contents. You won't need this again, so feel free to use any value. Also note the addition of oci.config. profile – this tells Micronaut which profile in your local CLI configuration to use for the OCI SDK. Stick with "DEFAULT."

Next, make a run/debug configuration for localadb that sets the proper values (Figure 8-1).

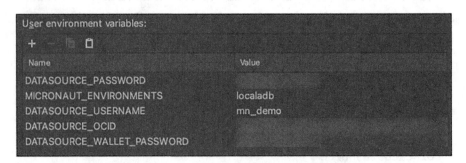

Figure 8-1. *Adding a run/debug configuration for the local environment*

We can now test out the automatic wallet download by running this new configuration. Note that the Liquibase script will create the necessary tables on the Autonomous DB instance. You'll also see some additional log output related to the automatic wallet download and configuration. After a few seconds, the app will be up and running, but this time connected to the Autonomous DB instance in the cloud!

Micronaut (v3.0.2)

11:56:42.720 [main] INFO i.m.context.env.DefaultEnvironment -
Established active environments: [test]
11:56:43.516 [main] INFO com.oracle.bmc.Services - Registering
new service: Services.BasicService(serviceName=DATABASE,
serviceEndpointPrefix=database, serviceEndpointTemplate=htt
ps://*database.{region}.{secondLevelDomain}*)

    11:56:44.005 [main] INFO c.o.b.h.s.i.BouncyCastleHelper -
    Instantiated provider: org.bouncycastle.jce.provider.
    BouncyCastleProvider
    11:56:44.092 [main] INFO c.oracle.bmc.http.
    ApacheConfigurator - Setting connector provider to
    ApacheConnectorProvider
    11:56:44.206 [main] INFO com.oracle.bmc.util.
    JavaRuntimeUtils - Determined JRE version *as* Unknown
    11:56:44.206 [main] WARN c.oracle.bmc.http.
    ApacheConfigurator - Using an unknown runtime, calls
    may not work
    11:56:44.250 [main] INFO com.oracle.bmc.Region -
    Loaded service 'DATABASE' endpoint mappings:
    {US_PHOENIX_1=https://*database.us-phoenix-1.*
    oraclecloud.com}
11:56:44.250 [main] INFO c.oracle.bmc.database.
DatabaseClient - Setting endpoint to https://*database.us-*
phoenix-1.oraclecloud.com

    11:56:44.604 [main] WARN c.oracle.bmc.database.
    DatabaseClient - generateAutonomousDatabaseWallet

returns a stream, please make sure to close the
stream to avoid any indefinite hangs
11:56:44.604 [main] WARN c.oracle.bmc.database.
DatabaseClient - ApacheConnectionClosingStrategy set to
org.glassfish.jersey.apache.connector.ApacheConnection
ClosingStrategy$ImmediateClosingStrategy@3d8b319e. For
large streams with partial reads of stream, please use
ImmediateClosingStrategy. For small streams with partial
reads of stream, please use GracefulClosingStrategy. More
info *in* ApacheConnectorProperties
11:56:45.106 [main] INFO com.oracle.bmc.ClientRuntime -
Using SDK: Oracle-JavaSDK/2.3.0
11:56:45.106 [main] INFO com.oracle.bmc.ClientRuntime -
User agent set to: Oracle-JavaSDK/2.3.0 (Mac OS X/10.16;
Java/11.0.5; OpenJDK 64-Bit Server VM/11.0.5+10)
11:56:47.607 [main] WARN c.o.bmc.http.internal.
ResponseHelper - Wrapping response stream into
auto closeable stream, *do* disable *this*, pleaseuse
ResponseHelper.shouldAutoCloseResponseInputStream(*false*)
11:56:48.570 [main] INFO i.m.o.a.j.OracleWalletArchiveProv
ider - Using *default* serviceAlias: demodb_high
Oct 19, 2021 11:56:54 AM liquibase.lockservice
INFO: Successfully acquired change log lock
Oct 19, 2021 11:56:54 AM liquibase.changelog
INFO: Creating database history table with name: MN_DEMO.
DATABASECHANGELOG
Oct 19, 2021 11:56:54 AM liquibase.changelog
INFO: Reading from MN_DEMO.DATABASECHANGELOG
Oct 19, 2021 11:56:55 AM liquibase.changelog
INFO: Table users created
Oct 19, 2021 11:56:55 AM liquibase.changelog

```
INFO: ChangeSet db/changelog/01-create-user-table.
xml::01::toddrsharp ran successfully in 282ms
Oct 19, 2021 11:56:55 AM liquibase.lockservice
INFO: Successfully released change log lock
Oct 19, 2021 11:56:56 AM liquibase.lockservice
INFO: Successfully acquired change log lock
Oct 19, 2021 11:57:06 AM liquibase.changelog
INFO: Reading from MN_DEMO.DATABASECHANGELOG
Oct 19, 2021 11:57:07 AM liquibase.lockservice
INFO: Successfully released change log lock
11:57:07.843 [main] INFO  io.micronaut.runtime.Micronaut -
Startup completed in 25243ms. Server Running: http://
localhost:25614
```

Now let's set up our "production" datasource.

Configure the Production Datasource

We'll need to add another new configuration file, so create a new file
in src/main/resources called application-oraclecloud.yml. Make
sure you use that exact name, because Micronaut supports environment
detection and can detect when your application is running on Oracle
Cloud and will load your environment-specific configuration accordingly.
That means that we can specify config variables that only apply to a
particular environment. Populate your new application-oraclecloud.
yml file like so:

```
datasources:
  default:
    driverClassName: oracle.jdbc.driver.OracleDriver
    connectionFactoryClassName: oracle.jdbc.pool.
    OracleDataSource
```

```
      ocid: ${DATASOURCE_OCID}
      walletPassword: ${DATASOURCE_WALLET_PASSWORD}
      username: ${DATASOURCE_USERNAME}
      password: ${DATASOURCE_PASSWORD}
      schema-generate: NONE
      dialect: ORACLE
oci:
  config:
    instance-principal:
      enabled: true
```

Note that we changed the oci config block here. We're going to use instance principal authentication instead of relying on an OCI config file when we deploy to the cloud. You'll want to make sure this is properly configured[2] before you try to deploy the app.

At this point, we could pass our credentials into the app at runtime via GitHub secrets, but that would result in our credentials being visible in the Bash history of the instance. A better idea would be to use the OCI Vault to store our credentials in an encrypted manner and take advantage of the Micronaut integration[3] for OCI Vaults to retrieve and decrypt the credentials at runtime.

First, create a vault secret corresponding to the credentials that we need at runtime. An overview of creating vault secrets is outside of the scope of this book, so if you're not familiar with the process, check out the OCI documentation.[4] Create a vault containing secrets that are named as

---

[2] https://docs.oracle.com/en-us/iaas/Content/Identity/Tasks/
callingservicesfrominstances.htm
[3] https://micronaut-projects.github.io/micronaut-oracle-cloud/snapshot/
guide/#vault
[4] https://docs.oracle.com/en-us/iaas/Content/KeyManagement/Concepts/
keyoverview.htm

follows (the naming is important, as Micronaut will create configuration variables that match the names exactly):

- DATASOURCE_OCID

- DATASOURCE_PASSWORD

- DATASOURCE_USERNAME

- DATASOURCE_WALLET_PASSWORD

Here's how that looks in the OCI console when viewing the vault (Figure 8-2).

Figure 8-2. *The list of secrets in the OCI console*

Next, add a dependency to `build.gradle`:

```
implementation("io.micronaut.oraclecloud:micronaut-oraclecloud-vault:2.0.3")
```

Because we want the secrets to be available in our `application.yml` file, we need to retrieve them before that file is processed. We can achieve this by creating a new file in the `/src/main/resources` directory called `bootstrap.yml`.

Populate the bootstrap file as follows. We're simply enabling the configuration client for bootstrapped applications here:

```
micronaut:
  config-client:
    enabled: true
```

Next, we'll create a `bootstrap-oraclecloud.yml` file that will be run when the app is deployed to Oracle Cloud. We'll need to enter the vault OCID, as well as the OCID of the compartment that the secrets were created in. It's very important that we add our OCI-specific configuration here, so that the secrets client can properly construct an authentication provider. Remember, the settings in your `application.yml` file will not yet be loaded!

```
oci:
  config:
    instance-principal:
      enabled: true
  vault:
    config:
      enabled: true
    vaults:
      - ocid: ocid1.vault.oc1.phx...
        compartment-ocid: ocid1.compartment.oc1...
```

Hint   Just like with our `application.yml` files, we can specify environment-specific `bootstrap-[env].yml` files that will only apply to the given environment.

And that's it! The credentials that we need for our datasource will be encrypted and properly injected at runtime since we named the secrets the same as the environment variable values that we used previously.

After pushing the changes, your pipeline job should execute successfully (Figure 8-3).

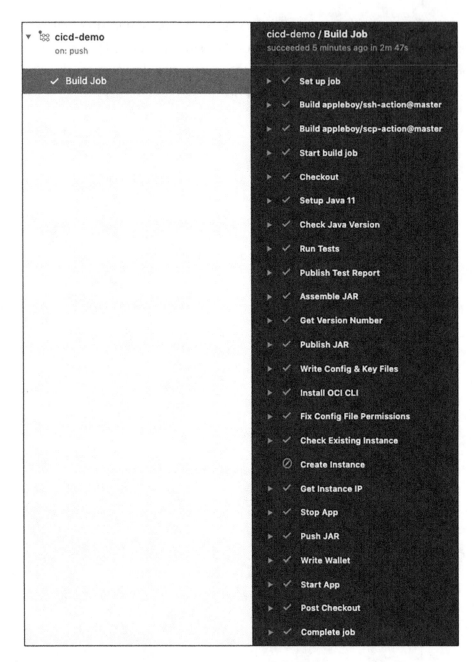

Figure 8-3. The new build output

If you SSH into the VM and look at the output log, you should see something similar to the following. Notice that the secrets are retrieved and injected, and our Liquibase migration has been properly run against our production Autonomous DB instance (some log entries have been removed for brevity):

```
11:26:47.630 [main] INFO  i.m.context.DefaultBeanContext -
Reading Startup environment from bootstrap.yml
[removed for brevity]
11:26:51.179 [main] TRACE i.m.o.d.v.OracleCloudVaultConfigurati
onClient - Retrieved secret: DATASOURCE_WALLET_PASSWORD
11:26:51.371 [main] TRACE i.m.o.d.v.OracleCloudVaultConfigurati
onClient - Retrieved secret: DATASOURCE_USERNAME
11:26:51.558 [main] TRACE i.m.o.d.v.OracleCloudVaultConfigurati
onClient - Retrieved secret: DATASOURCE_PASSWORD
11:26:51.743 [main] TRACE i.m.o.d.v.OracleCloudVaultConfigurati
onClient - Retrieved secret: DATASOURCE_OCID
11:26:51.744 [main] DEBUG i.m.o.d.v.OracleCloudVaultConfigurat
ionClient - 4 secrets where retrieved from Oracle Cloud Vault
with OCID: ocid1.vault.oc1.phx...
11:26:51.929 [main] INFO  i.m.d.c.c.DistributedPropertySourceLo
cator - Resolved 1 configuration sources from client: composite
ConfigurationClient(Retrieves secrets from Oracle Cloud vaults)
[removed for brevity]
11:26:52.302 [main] TRACE i.m.o.a.j.h.HikariPoolConfigurationLi
stener - Retrieving Oracle Wallet for DataSource [default]
11:26:52.304 [main] WARN  c.oracle.bmc.database.
DatabaseClient - generateAutonomousDatabaseWallet returns a
stream, please make sure to close the stream to avoid any
indefinite hangs
[removed for brevity]
```

```
11:26:56.146 [main] INFO  com.zaxxer.hikari.HikariDataSource -
HikariPool-1 - Starting...
11:26:57.647 [main] INFO  com.zaxxer.hikari.HikariDataSource -
HikariPool-1 - Start completed.
Oct 21, 2021 11:26:57 AM liquibase.database
Oct 21, 2021 11:26:58 AM liquibase.lockservice
INFO: Successfully acquired change log lock
Oct 21, 2021 11:27:10 AM liquibase.changelog
INFO: Reading from MN_DEMO.DATABASECHANGELOG
Oct 21, 2021 11:27:10 AM liquibase.lockservice
INFO: Successfully released change log lock
Oct 21, 2021 11:27:10 AM liquibase.database
Oct 21, 2021 11:27:11 AM liquibase.lockservice
INFO: Successfully acquired change log lock
Oct 21, 2021 11:27:18 AM liquibase.changelog
INFO: Reading from MN_DEMO.DATABASECHANGELOG
Oct 21, 2021 11:27:19 AM liquibase.lockservice
INFO: Successfully released change log lock
11:27:19.532 [main] INFO  io.micronaut.runtime.Micronaut -
Startup completed in 32193ms. Server Running: http://
localhost:8080
```

You can confirm the deployment with a few cURL commands:

```
curl -s \
    -H "Content-Type: application/json" \
    -X POST \
    -d '{"firstName":"todd", "lastName":"sharp", "email":
    "me@ohmy.com", "age":42}' \
    http://129.146.98.229:8080/hello/ | jq
```

This will create and return the new user object:

```
{
  "id": "69aedb66-d44a-41e2-8938-8c378217817e",
  "firstName": "todd",
  "lastName": "sharp",
  "age": 42,
  "email": "me@ohmy.com"
}
```

And here's how to retrieve that user by ID:

```
curl -s http://129.146.98.229:8080/hello/69aedb66-
d44a-41e2-8938-8c378217817e | jq
```

This returns the same user object:

```
{
  "id": "69aedb66-d44a-41e2-8938-8c378217817e",
  "firstName": "todd",
  "lastName": "sharp",
  "age": 42,
  "email": "me@ohmy.com"
}
```

TL;DR

In this chapter we created an Autonomous DB instance, configured our
app to automatically download our Autonomous DB wallet, and modified
our GitHub Actions pipeline to write our wallet to our production VM. We
then created a production-specific datasource configuration and modified
our "Start App" step to pass our DB password to the application when
launching it.

Next

In the next chapter, we'll switch gears and look at deploying our microservice application as a Docker container.

Source Code

The source code for this chapter can be found at `https://github.com/recursivecodes/cicd-demo/tree/part-8`.

CHAPTER 9

Deploying the Microservice as a Docker Container

Welcome to the penultimate chapter in this journey about continuous integration and continuous deployment. So far in this book, we have gone over a copious number of topics related to building and automated testing and deploying of a microservice using many popular tools in the Java and open source ecosystem. Honestly, there is not much left to talk about as it relates to the basics of continuous integration and deployment of microservices. There is however one more topic that we would be remiss to not mention, and that is building and deploying our microservice as a Docker container onto a Kubernetes cluster. It's not terribly complicated to do this, but we'll break this last topic up into two separate blog chapters. In this chapter we'll focus on building our Docker container.

© Todd Raymond Sharp 2022
T. R. Sharp, *Introducing Micronaut*, https://doi.org/10.1007/978-1-4842-8290-8_9

The Dockerfile

When we created our Micronaut project, you may have noticed that our build.gradle script includes a plugin with the ID io.micronaut. application. This is the Micronaut Gradle plugin,[1] and it adds some very helpful tasks that we can use to help with our Docker build.

The first task we'll look at is the dockerfile task. This task will generate a Dockerfile that we can use to build our container. We just need to specify a few items – the base image that we want to use and the ports that we want to expose. Open up your build.gradle and add this task to the bottom:

```
dockerfile {
    baseImage("adoptopenjdk/openjdk11:adoptopenjdk/openjdk11:
    jdk-11.0.11_9-alpine")
    exportPorts(8080)
}
```

Run it with ./gradlew dockerfile. Observe the output in your console:

```
> Task :dockerfile
Dockerfile written to: /Users/trsharp/Projects/apress/cicd-
demo/build/docker/Dockerfile
```

Now look at the generated Dockerfile:

```
FROM adoptopenjdk/openjdk11-openj9:jdk-11.0.11_9_openj9-0.26.0-
alpine-slim
WORKDIR /home/app
COPY layers/libs /home/app/libs
COPY layers/resources /home/app/resources
COPY layers/application.jar /home/app/application.jar
EXPOSE 8080
ENTRYPOINT ["java", "-jar", "/home/app/application.jar"]
```

---

[1] https://github.com/micronaut-projects/micronaut-gradle-plugin

We see here that the task generated a Dockerfile that is based on the image that we specified. It copies the resources and JAR file into it, exposes our port, and defines an ENTRYPOINT that launches the application. Nice!

Preparing to Build the Docker Image

We're going to need a Docker registry to store our Docker images. You can use Docker Hub if you'd like, but a great option for hosting Docker images on Oracle Cloud is the Oracle Cloud Infrastructure Registry (OCIR). If you have not yet configured OCIR for your tenancy, do so now before we move forward.

Tip!   Check out "The Complete Guide to Getting Up and Running with Docker and Kubernetes on the Oracle Cloud" for help getting prepared for Docker and Kubernetes! It can be found at `https://blogs.oracle.com/developers/the-complete-guide-to-getting-up-and-running-with-docker-and-kubernetes-on-the-oracle-cloud`.

Building the Docker Image

Now that we have a Dockerfile, we need to build it. Let's add another task definition to our build.gradle that specifies an image name that we want our image to be tagged with when we build it:

```
dockerBuild {
    images = ["phx.ocir.io/[your repo]/cicd-demo/cicd-
    demo:latest"]
}
```

To build our image, first make sure your JAR file is built locally with `./gradlew assemble` and then run

`./gradlew dockerBuild`

You'll notice that the output from running this Gradle task looks almost identical to running a Docker build natively:

```
$ ./gradlew dockerBuild

> Task :dockerBuild
Building image using context '/Users/trsharp/Projects/apress/
cicd-demo/build/docker'.
Using Dockerfile '/Users/trsharp/Projects/apress/cicd-demo/
build/docker/Dockerfile'
Using images 'phx.ocir.io/[your repo]/cicd-demo/cicd-
demo:latest'.
Step 1/7 : FROM adoptopenjdk/openjdk11-openj9:jdk-11.0.11_9_
openj9-0.26.0-alpine-slim
---> 7a582d82e0ae
Step 2/7 : WORKDIR /home/app
---> Running in 4a8bc413432c
Removing intermediate container 4a8bc413432c
---> 5d2986ff618f
Step 3/7 : COPY layers/libs /home/app/libs
---> ae712c41bf51
Step 4/7 : COPY layers/resources /home/app/resources
---> 96dedbe0f364
Step 5/7 : COPY layers/application.jar /home/app/
application.jar
---> 98d36d3c4314
Step 6/7 : EXPOSE 8080
```

```
---> Running in d3e85b5c36f3
Removing intermediate container d3e85b5c36f3
---> 9cff8ce9dbb9
Step 7/7 : ENTRYPOINT ["java", "-jar", "/home/app/
application.jar"]
---> Running in 80a5362b3372
Removing intermediate container 80a5362b3372
---> dd25306e27ce
Successfully built dd25306e27ce
Successfully tagged phx.ocir.io/[your repo]/cicd-demo/cicd-
demo:latest
Created image with ID 'dd25306e27ce'.
```

Running the Docker Build Locally

Before we can run this image, we need to set some environment variables
for our credentials so that we can pass them into the running container.
Since I'm on a Mac, I need to make sure that I use the special docker.for.
mac.localhost host name for my local version of Oracle XE:

```
export DATASOURCE_PASSWORD=Str0ng_Pa\$\$w0rd
export MICRONAUT_ENVIRONMENTS=dev
export DATASOURCE_USERNAME=mn_demo
export DATASOURCE_URL=jdbc:oracle:thin:@docker.for.mac.
localhost:1521/XEPDB1
```

Now we can run it with

```
$ docker run -d \
    --env DATASOURCE_USERNAME \
    --env DATASOURCE_PASSWORD \
    --env DATASOURCE_URL \
```

```
--env MICRONAUT_ENVIRONMENTS \
-p 8080:8080 \
phx.ocir.io/toddrsharp/cicd-demo/cicd-demo:latest
```

Modifying the Build

Now that we've configured Docker and tested that it builds properly, we need to modify our GitHub Actions workflow to automate these tasks and push the resulting Docker image to our OCIR repo. To prepare for that, we'll need to create two more secrets in GitHub, one for our OCIR_ USERNAME (in the tenancy/username format) and one for the token called OCIR_PASSWORD (Figure 9-1).

Figure 9-1. *Adding new secrets to the GitHub repository*

Hint   If you don't have a need for anything related to deploying to a VM and would only like to deploy to Docker, you can remove all the previous steps related to the compute instance deployment now.

Next, add a step to log in to OCIR. This step will use the docker/login-action@v1 action to perform the login. Substitute your appropriate URL if you are not using the PHX region!

```
- name: 'Login To OCIR'
  uses: docker/login-action@v1
  with:
    registry: phx.ocir.io
    username: ${{secrets.OCIR_USERNAME}}
    password: ${{secrets.OCIR_PASSWORD}}
```

Now let's do the same ./gradlew dockerfile and ./gradlew dockerBuild commands that we used to test the Docker build locally in our pipeline:

```
- name: 'Docker Build'
  run: |
    ./gradlew dockerfile
    ./gradlew dockerBuild
```

And finally, push that image to OCIR:

```
- name: 'Docker Push'
  run: |
    ./gradlew dockerPush
```

Observe your build on GitHub, and it should complete successfully (Figure 9-2).

Figure 9-2. *The new build output*

We can confirm this by checking our OCIR and observing that the Docker image has been pushed to our repository (Figure 9-3).

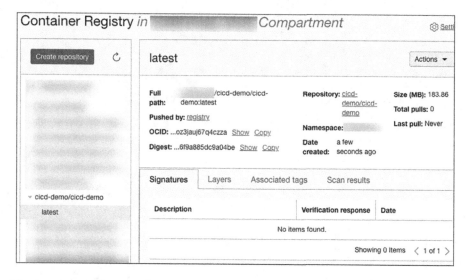

Figure 9-3. *The Docker image details in OCIR*

TL;DR

In this chapter we modified our GitHub Actions workflow to build a Docker image that contains our microservice and pushed that image to our OCIR.

Next

In the next chapter, we'll deploy our microservice Docker image to a Kubernetes cluster on Oracle Cloud.

Source Code

The source code for this chapter can be found at https://github.com/recursivecodes/cicd-demo/tree/part-9.

CHAPTER 10

Deploying the Microservice Docker Container to Kubernetes

Welcome to the final entry in this book where we have taken a ground-up approach to building, testing, and deploying a microservice for the cloud in an automated manner. In this final chapter, we're going to deploy our Docker container that contains our microservice application to a Kubernetes cluster on Oracle Cloud. It's not a complicated task, but it does have some noteworthy things to keep in mind, so let's dig in!

You probably already have a Kubernetes cluster configured in your cloud environment, but if not, here are a few resources to help you get one up and running quickly:

- `https://blogs.oracle.com/developers/the-complete-guide-to-getting-up-and-running-with-docker-and-kubernetes-on-the-oracle-cloud`

- `www.youtube.com/watch?v=lDxVQxmzdWo`

© Todd Raymond Sharp 2022
T. R. Sharp, *Introducing Micronaut*, https://doi.org/10.1007/978-1-4842-8290-8_10

Create a Service Account

Before we can use kubectl in our pipeline, we need to configure a service account on our Kubernetes cluster so that our GitHub Actions pipeline has the proper authority to issue commands to our cluster. There is a helpful guide in our online docs,[1] but we'll walk through the steps needed to configure this in the following. We're going to create a service account that has a non-expiring token that can execute commands from the pipeline.

Step 1

Create the service account that uses the name cicd-demo and a cluster role binding for that service account:

```
$ kubectl -n kube-system create serviceaccount cicd-demo
$ kubectl create clusterrolebinding cicd-demo-binding
--clusterrole=cluster-admin --serviceaccount=kube-
system:cicd-demo
```

Step 2

Grab the name of the token that was created for the service account. Then get the token:

```
$ TOKENNAME=`kubectl -n kube-system get serviceaccount/cicd-
demo -o jsonpath='{.secrets[0].name}'`
$ TOKEN=`kubectl -n kube-system get secret $TOKENNAME -o
jsonpath='{.data.token}'| base64 --decode`
```

---

[1] https://docs.cloud.oracle.com/en-us/iaas/Content/ContEng/Tasks/
contengaddingserviceaccttoken.htm

Step 3

On your local machine, add the service account and token to your local config file by executing

```
$ kubectl config set-credentials cicd-demo --token=$TOKEN
```

Step 4

Note   **Do not skip this step; it is crucial!** Set the current context to be the service account user we created in step 1. You can change this later on after you export your config, but it is important that this is done before step 5.

```
$ kubectl config set-context –current --user=cicd-demo
```

Step 5

Export a base64 representation of your local Kubernetes config and copy to your clipboard:

```
$ more ~/.kube/config | base64 | pbcopy
```

Step 6

Create a GitHub secret containing the base64 representation of your config (Figure 10-1).

Add a new secret

Name

OKE_KUBE_CONFIG

Value

YXBpVmVyc2lvbjogdjEKY2x1c3RlcnM6Ci0gY2x1c3RlcjoKICAglGNlcnRpZmljYXRlLWF1d...

Add secret

Figure 10-1. *Adding a GitHub secret with the Kubernetes config*

We can now start using the kubectl GitHub action[2] in our pipeline to work with our OKE cluster!

Create Kubernetes Deployment Configuration

The first thing we're going to need to create is a deployment configuration for our microservice. This involves two things: an app.yaml to define our deployment and the associated service and a secret to contain our credentials. If you've been following along with this book, you know that we've already got the secret values in our GitHub repository (we created them in Chapter 8), so we just need to create our secret in our cluster from that value.

---

[2] https://github.com/marketplace/actions/kubernetes-cli-kubectl

Create a Secret

Let's add a step to our build to create the secret. We can do this directly via kubectl without writing a config file, so add a step to do that:

```
- name: 'Create Password Secret'
  uses: steebchen/kubectl@@v2.0.0master
  with:
    config: ${{secrets.OKE_KUBE_CONFIG}}
    command: "create secret generic cicd-secrets
    --from-literal=dbUsername='${{secrets.DATASOURCE_
    USERNAME}}' --from-literal=dbPassword='${{secrets.
    DATASOURCE_PASSWORD}}' --from-literal=dbWalletPasswo
    rd='${{secrets.DATASOURCE_WALLET_PASSWORD}}' --from-
    literal=dbOcid='${{secrets.DATASOURCE_OCID}}' --save-config
    --dry-run -o yaml | kubectl apply -f -"
```

Create Deployment YAML

Next, create a file at k8s/app.yaml relative to your project root and populate it with the service and deployment definition. Make sure that the image value points to the proper location where your Docker image is being stored (see Chapter 9). Notice that we're using an imagePullPolicy of Always, which means regardless of the tag on our Docker image, Kubernetes will always pull a new version instead of using a locally cached image. If you're new to Kubernetes, make sure you create a secret containing your registry credentials[3] and use that as your imagePullSecrets value.

---

[3] https://kubernetes.io/docs/tasks/configure-pod-container/
pull-image-private-registry/

Also notice the values we're passing as environment variables to the deployment are being pulled from the secret that we just created:

```
kind: Service
apiVersion: v1
metadata:
  name: cicd-demo-app
  labels:
    app: cicd_demo
spec:
  type: LoadBalancer
  selector:
    app: cicd-demo-app
  ports:
    - name: http
      protocol: TCP
      port: 80
      targetPort: 8080
---
kind: Deployment
apiVersion: apps/v1
metadata:
  name: cicd-demo-app
  labels:
    app: cicd-demo-app
    version: v1
spec:
  selector:
    matchLabels:
      app: cicd-demo-app
  replicas: 1
```

```
template:
  metadata:
    labels:
      app: cicd-demo-app
      version: v1
  spec:
    containers:
      - name: cicd-demo-app
        image: phx.ocir.io/[redacted]/cicd-demo/cicd-
        demo:latest
        env:
          - name: DATASOURCE_OCID
            valueFrom:
              secretKeyRef:
                name: cicd-secrets
                key: dbOcid
          - name: DATASOURCE_USERNAME
            valueFrom:
              secretKeyRef:
                name: cicd-secrets
                key: dbUsername
          - name: DATASOURCE_PASSWORD
            valueFrom:
              secretKeyRef:
                name: cicd-secrets
                key: dbPassword
          - name: DATASOURCE_WALLET_PASSWORD
            valueFrom:
              secretKeyRef:
                name: cicd-secrets
                key: dbWalletPassword
```

```
      imagePullPolicy: Always
      ports:
         - containerPort: 8080
   imagePullSecrets:
     - name: regcred
```

Add a Deployment Step

Now let's add a step to our pipeline to perform the deployment:

```
- name: 'Deploy To Kubernetes'
  uses: steebchen/kubectl@v2.0.0
  with:
    config: ${{secrets.OKE_KUBE_CONFIG}}
    command: apply -f ./k8s/app.yaml
```

Kill an Existing Pod

Finally, add a step to grab the most recent pod in this deployment and kill it. This will ensure that our deployment is running the latest and greatest Docker image that was pushed to OCIR during this build:

```
- name: 'Kill Pod'
  uses: steebchen/kubectl@v2.0.0
  with:
    config: ${{secrets.OKE_KUBE_CONFIG}}
    command: delete pod $(kubectl get pod -l app=cicd-demo-app
    -o jsonpath="{.items[0].metadata.name}")
```

The Final Build

Once we commit and push our latest changes, we can observe the final
build in this book and confirm that it completed successfully (Figure 10-2).

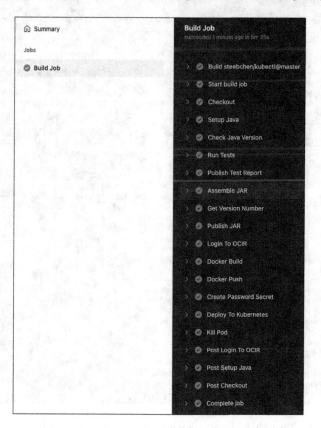

Figure 10-2. *The final build output*

We can then view our pod logs in the Kubernetes dashboard to confirm
Liquibase executed and our application has started up (Figure 10-3).

```
Logs from cicd-demo-app ▾ in cicd-demo-app-b56988f8f-75nkn ▾

15:12:04.316        INFO  c.oracle.bmc.http.ApacheConfigurator  - Setting connect
15:12:04.511        INFO  com.oracle.bmc.util.JavaRuntimeUtils  - Determined JRE
15:12:04.511        WARN  c.oracle.bmc.http.ApacheConfigurator  - Using an unknow
15:12:04.529        INFO  c.oracle.bmc.http.ApacheConfigurator  - Setting connect
15:12:04.530        WARN  c.oracle.bmc.http.ApacheConfigurator  - Using an unknow
15:12:04.545        INFO  com.oracle.bmc.Region - Loaded service 'DATABASE' endp
1.oraclecloud.com}
15:12:04.545        INFO  c.oracle.bmc.database.DatabaseClient  - Setting endpoin
15:12:04.731        TRACE i.m.o.a.j.h.HikariPoolConfigurationListener - Retrievi
15:12:04.733        WARN  c.oracle.bmc.database.DatabaseClient  - generateAutonom
stream to avoid any indefinite hangs
15:12:04.733        WARN  c.oracle.bmc.database.DatabaseClient  - ApacheConnectio
org.glassfish.jersey.apache.connector.ApacheConnectionClosingStrategy$ImmediateC
stream, please use ImmediateClosingStrategy. For small streams with partial read
ApacheConnectorProperties
15:12:04.924        INFO  c.o.b.a.i.X509FederationClient  - Refreshing session ke
15:12:05.527        INFO  c.o.b.a.i.X509FederationClient  - Getting security toke
15:12:05.631        INFO  com.oracle.bmc.ClientRuntime  - Using SDK: Oracle-JavaS
15:12:05.632        INFO  com.oracle.bmc.ClientRuntime  - User agent set to: Orac
Eclipse OpenJ9 VM/openj9-0.26.0)
15:12:07.437        WARN  c.o.bmc.http.internal.ResponseHelper  - Wrapping respon
ResponseHelper.shouldAutoCloseResponseInputStream(false)
15:12:08.329        INFO  i.m.o.a.j.OracleWalletArchiveProvider  - Using default
15:12:08.997        INFO  com.zaxxer.hikari.HikariDataSource  - HikariPool-1 - St
15:12:09.748        INFO  com.zaxxer.hikari.HikariDataSource  - HikariPool-1 - St
Oct 20, 2021 3:12:10 PM liquibase.database
INFO: Could not set remarks reporting on OracleDatabase: com.zaxxer.hikari.pool.
Oct 20, 2021 3:12:10 PM liquibase.lockservice
INFO: Successfully acquired change log lock
Oct 20, 2021 3:12:15 PM liquibase.changelog
INFO: Reading from MN_DEMO.DATABASECHANGELOG
Oct 20, 2021 3:12:15 PM liquibase.lockservice
INFO: Successfully released change log lock
Oct 20, 2021 3:12:15 PM liquibase.database
INFO: Could not set remarks reporting on OracleDatabase: com.zaxxer.hikari.pool.
Oct 20, 2021 3:12:15 PM liquibase.lockservice
INFO: Successfully acquired change log lock
Oct 20, 2021 3:12:16 PM liquibase.changelog
INFO: Reading from MN_DEMO.DATABASECHANGELOG
Oct 20, 2021 3:12:16 PM liquibase.lockservice
INFO: Successfully released change log lock
15:12:17.516        INFO  io.micronaut.runtime.Micronaut  - Startup completed in
```

Figure 10-3. *The Kubernetes pod log*

Now grab the newly created service IP address (Figure 10-4).

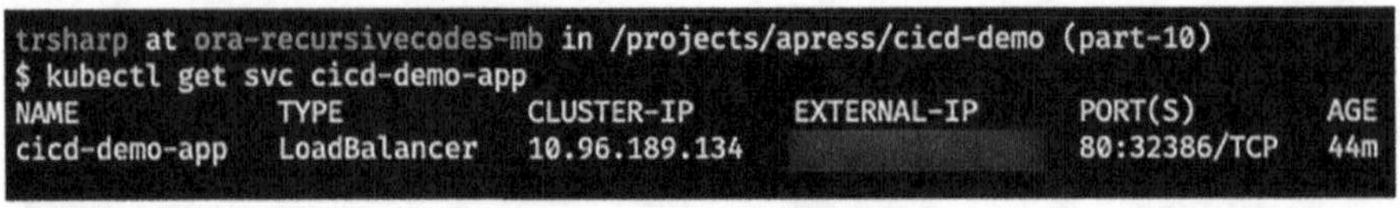

```
trsharp at ora-recursivecodes-mb in /projects/apress/cicd-demo (part-10)
$ kubectl get svc cicd-demo-app
NAME            TYPE            CLUSTER-IP      EXTERNAL-IP     PORT(S)       AGE
cicd-demo-app   LoadBalancer    10.96.189.134                   80:32386/TCP  44m
```

Figure 10-4. *The Kubernetes service details*

And confirm by sending a POST request to create a new user:

```
curl -s \
    -H "Content-Type: application/json" \
    -X POST \
    -d '{"firstName":"todd", "lastName":"sharp", "email":
    "me@ohmy.com", "age":42}' \
    http://[service IP]/hello | jq
{

    "id": "a936faf4-4092-416b-bdd5-b15238aed42c",
    "firstName": "todd",
    "lastName": "sharp",
    "age": 42,
    "email": "me@ohmy.com"
}
```

TL;DR

We've deployed our microservice as a Docker container in our OKE Kubernetes cluster!

Next

Unfortunately, our pilgrimage into the expansive, electrifying universe of continuous integration and continuous deployment has come to an exciting conclusion! I hope you have learned everything you possibly wanted to about automated deployments and have picked up some valuable tools that can make your application deployment rapid and painless when working with Oracle Cloud.

If you have any feedback or would like to connect with me to suggest future content ideas or discuss anything Oracle Cloud or development related, feel free to connect with me on Twitter[4] or YouTube.[5] Thank you for reading!

Source Code

The source code for this chapter can be found at `https://github.com/recursivecodes/cicd-demo/tree/part-10`.

---

[4] `https://twitter.com/recursivecodes`
[5] `https://youtube.com/c/recursivecodes`

Index

© Todd Raymond Sharp 2022
T. R. Sharp, *Introducing Micronaut*, https://doi.org/10.1007/978-1-4842-8290-8

Printed in the United States
by Baker & Taylor Publisher Services